SCHOOL OF THE PROPHET

SCHOOL OF THE PROPHET

Joseph Smith Learns the First Principles, 1820–1830

Richard E. Bennett

DESERET BOOK

Salt Lake City, Utah

Visit us at DeseretBook.com

Library of Congress Cataloging-in-Publication Data

Bennett, Richard Edmond, 1946–
School of the prophet : Joseph Smith learns the first principles, 1820–1830 / Richard E. Bennett.
p. cm.
Includes bibliographical references and index.
ISBN 978-1-59038-996-6 (hardbound : alk. paper)
1. Smith, Joseph, 1805–1844—Knowledge and learning. 2. Church of Jesus Christ of Latter-day Saints—Doctrines—History. I. Title.
BX8695.S6B425 2010
230'.93092—dc22 2010015665

Printed in the United States of America
Worldcolor, Fairfield, PA

10 9 8 7 6 5 4 3 2 1

To my loving parents,
Cliff and Evelyn,
and to my brother,
Gary—
a family of faith

CONTENTS

PREFACE

The origins of this book come from deep within my own experiences and challenges. I have devoted my professional career to teaching, researching, and writing Church history in as objective a way as possible. As a scholar and historian, I have made it a priority to think critically and objectively, to find the facts and to let those facts speak for themselves. Works of a more doctrinal, more interpretive nature I have tended to leave to others much more qualified and schooled in such matters than myself. Thus it is somewhat out of character for me to write an interpretation of early Church history through very doctrinal lenses. Nevertheless, I have tried to include in this work fresh, new historical information and insights to accompany my doctrinal interpretations.

Though an ardent student of Church history, I have always looked upon the miracle of the Restoration through more spiritual lenses. It has ever beckoned me to improve my life more than it has for me to accumulate a data bank of historical facts. From the time I first visited the Sacred Grove more than fifty years ago as part of a deeply devout, loving, and thoroughly converted family, I have believed in the validity of Joseph Smith's claim as prophet of this dispensation. Yet ironically, part of my motivation has been the continuing spate of works critical of the Prophet, works that portray him as a product of a broken psychology or a dysfunctional home, works dedicated to magnifying his faults and discrediting his claims. The proof for me has not been in the historical facts of the Restoration only but also in the confirmations of the Spirit and in the fruits of those who have followed Joseph Smith and his teachings.

I do not wish to suggest that my interpretation of these early years in Church history is something new or revolutionary or that it is the only way to look at and interpret these events. Nor do I presume in these matters to know and understand the mind and purposes of God. For me, this interpretation is something of a new paradigm, a somewhat different and very compelling way to understand the Restoration and what Joseph Smith was taught. Part of the inspiration for this work I attribute to my years of teaching Church history and the Doctrine and Covenants to classrooms full of spiritually sensitive students at Brigham Young University, for one cannot teach others without learning much more himself. So, too, my colleagues on the faculty of Religious Education remain an inspiration to me.

I also owe special thanks to my intrepid research assistant, Rebecca Monson, who, like a modern-day Oliver Cowdery, one day showed up at my office, offered her assistance to this work in particular, located many sources, and served cheerfully as my initial scribe. I wish also to thank Cyndi Hampshire for her splendid work in verifying and preparing the citations and final drafts,

Patty Smith for typing the original manuscript, and Bethany Lott for her work with other duties as assigned. Above all I wish to thank my loyal and loving wife, Patricia, for her constant support, inspiration, and encouragement. Without her and the support of our five wonderful children, this book could never have come to pass.

INTRODUCTION

The only and true doctrine of the Father,
and of the Son, and of the Holy Ghost.
2 Nephi 31:21

In 1865, President John Taylor spoke of the abiding importance of the first principles and ordinances of the gospel and of the role Joseph Smith played in bringing them forward: "Who told us that it was right to be baptized in the name of Jesus for the remission of sins? Who taught us it was right to receive the Holy Ghost by the laying on of hands? Who taught us that it was right that there should be an authority given by God to man to enable him to officiate legally in His name? . . . It was communicated to Joseph Smith by the opening of the heavens, by the ministering of Holy Angels, and by the voice of God. Until that voice was heard, until these communications were made known, the inhabitants of the world were wrapped in ignorance; they knew nothing about God nor the principles of eternity, nor the way to save themselves nor anybody else."[1]

Nothing else is as important to the core teachings of The

Church of Jesus Christ of Latter-day Saints as are the saving doctrines of faith in the Lord Jesus Christ, repentance, baptism by lawful authority from God, the conferring of the gift of the Holy Ghost by that same authority, and enduring to the end. These principles were so carefully impressed upon Joseph's mind—and in such perfect, instructional sequence—that by the time he wrote them down as the fourth article of faith in his well-known Wentworth Letter of 1842, they were far more than words; they had become part of his very being: "We believe that the first principles and ordinances of the Gospel are: first, Faith in the Lord Jesus Christ; second, Repentance; third, Baptism by immersion for the remission of sins; fourth, Laying on of hands for the gift of the Holy Ghost" (Articles of Faith 1:4).[2]

The restoration of the gospel of Jesus Christ was a deliberate process of continuing revelation and continuous personal development. What began in a grove of trees in upstate New York in the spring of 1820 would not result in the formation of the Church of Christ for another decade. The translation and publication of the Book of Mormon, the restoration of priesthood authority, and the preparation of a prophet would all take time. This ten-year incubation period would involve much personal preparation and the careful teaching of saving gospel principles, for it was essential that the message of the gospel be lived by the messenger of the gospel. To think otherwise is incongruous and incompatible with the essential integrity of the message of the Restoration. In the early years of the Restoration would come a divinely inspired apprenticeship of a young prophet, a careful schooling and tutoring in matters of deep and lasting importance. Joseph Smith, the first convert and first student of this "marvellous work and a wonder" (Isaiah 29:14; 2 Nephi 25:17), would need to be taught what he would later be called upon to teach. And nothing would be left to chance.

It was ever so. Moses underwent decades of preparation for his mission of leading the children of Israel to their promised land. From his days in Pharaoh's court to the burning bush and later to his return to Egypt to bring his people out of bondage, Moses was taught and prepared, chastened and challenged. Likewise, the apostle Peter, who had been called from his fishing boats to serve at Christ's side, learned much from his daily walk with the Savior. But even Peter, not yet the man of spiritual steel he would later become after receiving the gift of the Holy Ghost, denied his Master in his moment of greatest trial. Thereafter, in a pattern of careful teaching and forgiveness that the Lord wrought upon him, Peter never looked back. And neither did Samuel, Paul, Alma the Younger, and a host of other prophets. All of them required the careful tooling, tutoring, and refining of a greater power, and to the extent humanly possible, the lives of the prophets mirrored their message. So it would be now with Joseph Smith, the young boy of Palmyra.

Thus in addition to the First Vision, the bringing forth of the Book of Mormon, the restoration of the holy priesthood, and the accomplishment of other prerequisites for the reestablishment of the Church of Jesus Christ, the Lord also carefully and sequentially instructed the budding prophet Joseph Smith in the saving first principles and ordinances of the gospel—what Nephi termed "the doctrine of Christ" and "the only and true doctrine of the Father, and of the Son, and of the Holy Ghost" (2 Nephi 31:21). Joseph's instructions came in perfect order and from master teachers—in truth, from angels from on high and the Lord himself.

President Gordon B. Hinckley said: "To me the gospel is not

a great mass of theological jargon. It is a simple and beautiful and logical thing, with one quiet truth following another in orderly sequence. . . . God has revealed in this dispensation a great and marvelous and beautiful plan that motivates men and women to love their Creator and their Redeemer, to appreciate and serve one another, to walk in faith on the road that leads to immortality and eternal life."[3]

Of this same truth, President J. Reuben Clark taught: "The instructions came gradually, for his mind was finite, while the subject was infinite. So, as time went on, God revealed to the boy prophet the things he should know in order to restore and again build up the Church of Christ on earth. . . . Then began a long series of revelations from God to Joseph, sometimes in rapid succession, sometimes at considerable intervals, all for the guidance and building up of the Church, and for the instruction of the Saints in the principles of the Restored Gospel."[4]

One of the enduring truths of the restoration of the gospel is its lasting integrity as the miraculous power of Christ to transform the human soul. More than a package of principles and truths, it is the God-given power to bring men and women to Christ, to change not merely outlooks, patterns, and traditions but also habits, attitudes, and inclinations. Therefore, in the restoration of the gospel, there is as much a call to change personal dispositions as to harmonize past dispensations, to bring about a fulness of joy as to bring about the fulness of times. Essentially, the restoration of the gospel is more than a historical fact, although it is all of that; it is also a deeply personal matter of the soul.

The first principles speak to the deepest affections of our lives. When lived by, they become a lighthouse in the storms of our afflictions, the anchor to our intellectual wanderings and speculations, and the engine of our spiritual healing. To borrow from the words of William Wordsworth, they are

> *Truths that wake,*
> *To perish never;*
> *Which neither listlessness, nor mad endeavor,*
> *Nor Man nor Boy,*
> *Nor all that is at enmity with joy,*
> *Can utterly abolish or destroy!*[5]

Of the centrality of these principles and the necessity of conforming our lives to them, President Joseph F. Smith once declared: "Without [faith], repentance and baptism and the reception of the Holy Ghost, which constitute the new birth, we are not of the family of Christ, but are aliens, estranged from God and his laws, and in this fallen condition we shall remain, whether in the body or in the spirit, for time and for eternity, unless we render obedience to the plan devised in the heavens for the redemption and salvation of the human family."[6]

Hence God not only called and prepared a new prophet in the youthful Joseph Smith but likewise established in him a pattern for instruction and conversion. As with the calling of the apostle Paul, with whom Joseph often compared himself, Joseph's calling resulted from his conversion and grew out of his careful personal preparations.

And as with young Joseph, may it not also be with us? Church history is nothing if not instructive. As we study the patterns and progress of the Restoration, we as readers may come to recognize that a similar drama may be unfolding in our own lives, that we, too, are being carefully taught and prepared in these very same first principles and in the critical importance of abiding by them.

One last note before we begin. So much of a biographical nature has been written in recent years on the life of the Prophet Joseph Smith that one may well wonder if there is anything new or important left to say about him. Dan Vogel and Richard Bushman in their dramatically counterpoint interpretations of the Prophet from Palmyra, the former contending he was a "pious fraud" and the other asserting he was a legitimate American prophet, have forced us to reconsider the earlier arguments and interpretations of Donna and Marvin Hill, Fawn Brodie, John Henry Evans, and George Q. Cannon. Yet the contrasting contributions of Bushman and Vogel and the fervent, sometimes deeply emotional, responses to them have reinforced in my mind the conviction that the study of Joseph Smith's life and religious contributions is a fruitful field that continually beckons new generations to careful study and reflection. Too many defenders in the past have downplayed the value of historical analysis and contemporary documentation, whereas too many critics have derided the place of scriptural and prophetic authority. Both are necessary for believing Latter-day Saints. Consequently, my present purpose is not to attempt a full-length biography of Joseph Smith but to explore the pages of both Church history and holy writ to show how Joseph Smith was carefully and thoroughly taught the first principles and ordinances of the gospel between 1820 and 1830.

Chapter One

AND THUS BY FAITH, THEY DID LAY HOLD UPON EVERY GOOD THING

If any of you lack wisdom, let him ask of God, that giveth to all men liberally, and upbraideth not; and it shall be given him. But let him ask in faith, nothing wavering.

JAMES 1:5–6

The boy prophet Joseph Smith, unschooled in the religions of man, and his account of the First Vision demand our careful scrutiny. It is true that he lacked wisdom and that after reading from the Bible (James 1:5) he decided to pray and ask God which of all the churches was true. It had been prophesied that the Lord would one day raise up such a prophet to bring his people "to the knowledge of the covenants which I have made with [their] fathers" (2 Nephi 3:7). Likewise, in the economy of heaven, Joseph was foreordained to his work, and God, "knowing the calamity which should come upon the inhabitants of the earth," called upon his servant and "gave him commandments" (D&C 1:17).[1] Yet it is also true that faith precedes the miracle and that arguably the greatest miracle of the Restoration—the appearance of the Father and the Son to the boy prophet in 1820—required a demonstration of great faith. Thus our purpose will be to show that Joseph

Smith was prepared and taught the first principle of the gospel before he experienced the First Vision of the Restoration.

"Without Faith It Is Impossible to Please Him"

President J. Reuben Clark Jr. is reported to have said: "Faith is the antidote of fear, the eye that sees the invisible, the ear that hears the inaudible, the touch that feels the untouchable, the act that accomplishes the impossible."

If faith is a principle of power, then faith in the Lord Jesus Christ is a principle of hope, redemption, and eternal salvation. The apostle Paul described faith as "the substance of things hoped for, the evidence of things not seen" (Hebrews 11:1). Alma, when confronting a faithless Korihor—who had dismissed faith as "a foolish and a vain hope" and "a belief of things which are not so" (Alma 30:13, 16)—called on him and all others to "give place" for an "experiment" with faith, if only to desire to obtain it. This "true seed" of faith, if nurtured in earnest prayer and fervent hope, will begin to be discernible, will "swell within your breasts . . . [until] it beginneth to enlarge [the] soul; yea, it beginneth to enlighten [the] understanding, yea, it beginneth to be delicious." Alma then asked, "Is not this real?" (Alma 32:28, 33, 35). One might argue, therefore, that faith is neither foolishness nor "the effect of a frenzied mind" (Alma 30:16) but the ultimate reality.

Faith transcends emotions and is not a mere idle belief; rather, it is an attribute, a feeling, a reality of spiritual light and yearning hope, a force and a knowledge that quicken the mind while activating the soul. The Prophet Joseph Smith and Sidney Rigdon, in their *Lectures on Faith,* described it as "the principle of action in all intelligent beings."[2] Elder James E. Talmage said, "Faith is vivified, vitalized, living belief" that, even more than a mere possession of knowledge, changes our evil natures. And as one draws closer to God through faith, confidence in him increases, faith grows, and life trends ever upward.[3] Like a planted seed, faith can be discerned as it grows within, and when rooted in and pointed toward Christ, faith refines, elevates, educates, and transforms the soul. It is the principle of action and means by which we approach the divine, for "without faith it is impossible to please him" (Hebrews 11:6). It encompasses, as the prophet Ether wrote, "a more excellent hope" (Ether 12:32) filled with trust, foresight, and confidence, inevitably inspiring one to greater righteousness and obedience, whatever the cost. And because faith in Christ and sin are opposites, to sin knowingly is to "deny the faith" (D&C 42:23; 63:16).

A formidable mystery to the unbelieving, faith in Christ is the very opposite of gullibility, blind acceptance, or vacant hope. It is the very source of power to endure and overcome incredible pain, unwanted affliction, untold sorrows, nagging doubts, and intellectual scorn and derision, giving assurances when answers to the greatest questions of life and death seem nowhere to be found. Faith stands resolute, resilient, and resistant in the face of life's many wrongs, profound injustices, and cruel disappointments. It stands undaunted, unbowed, unyielding—the very rock and foundation of the Christian soul.

And faith cannot be unanswered. Of this truth the apostle Paul wrote: "By faith Abel offered unto God a more excellent sacrifice than Cain. . . . By faith Enoch was translated that he should not see death. . . . By faith Noah . . . prepared an ark. . . . By faith Abraham, when he was tried, offered up Isaac. . . . By faith Isaac blessed Jacob. . . . By faith Moses . . . refused to be called the son of Pharaoh's daughter. . . . By faith . . . the prophets . . . subdued kingdoms, wrought righteousness, obtained promises, stopped the mouths of lions, quenched the violence of fire, escaped the edge of the sword, out of weakness were made strong, waxed valiant in fight, turned to flight the armies of the aliens. Women received their dead raised to life again: and others were tortured . . . stoned . . . sawn asunder . . . slain with the sword: they wandered about in sheepskins and goatskins; being destitute, afflicted, tormented. (Of whom the world was not worthy:). . . . And these all, having obtained a good report through faith" (Hebrews 11:4–39).

Faith in Jehovah, the Man of Galilee and the risen Christ, is the activating force for good one reads about in the Old and New Testaments, in the Book of Mormon, and in all other scripture. It is the kind of faith that is most fulfilling, redeeming, and healing. To have this kind of faith, one must know, as Joseph Smith taught, that God actually exists, and one must have a "correct idea of his character, perfections, and attributes" and "an actual knowledge that the course of life which one is pursuing is according to his will."[4] By this kind of faith, the woman "diseased with an issue of blood twelve years" was healed by earnestly touching the hem of her Master's cloak (Matthew 9:20), Peter walked upon the sea (Matthew 14:29), the daughter of Jairus was raised from the dead (Mark 5:40–43), blind Bartimaeus received his sight (Mark 10:46–52), and Enos received a forgiveness of his sins (Enos 1:1–8). The Lord then said to Enos, "Whatsoever thing ye shall ask in faith, believing that ye shall receive in the name of Christ, ye shall receive it" (Enos 1:15).

There is a faith unto knowledge, a faith unto healing, and a "faith unto repentance" (Alma 34:15–17) that, in requiring the sacrifice of sin, is the power of reclamation and obedience, which eventually lead to a changed life and "a new creature" in Christ (2 Corinthians 5:17)—the rebirth the Savior promised his followers. Thus faith is the currency of testimony and the agent and impetus for permanent change and lasting transformation.

And faith leads to prayer and invigorates it, as Joseph Smith learned. Wrote the Prophet Joseph several years after the First Vision: "Remember that without asking we can receive nothing, . . . ask in faith, and ye shall receive such blessings as God sees fit to bestow upon you. Pray not with covetous hearts . . . but pray earnestly for the best gifts—fight the good fight of faith that ye may gain the crown which is laid up for those that endure faithful unto the end of their probation."[5]

Latter-day Saints are not alone in recognizing the life-changing power of faith in the Lord Jesus Christ. Billy Graham, a great evangelist of the twentieth century, spoke of the modern realities of this "'impossible' faith—with a God who is, with an Incarnation that is earthly and historical, with a salvation that is at cross-purposes with human nature, with a Resurrection that blasts apart the finality of death—is able to provide an alternative to the sifting, settling dust of death and through a new birth open the way to new life."[6] C. S. Lewis defined this faith as "the art of holding on to things your reason has once accepted, in spite of your changing moods. . . . Consequently one must train the habit of Faith. . . . Faith in Christ is the only thing to save you from despair . . . and out of that Faith in Him good actions must inevitably come."[7] And Pope Benedict XVI declared: "And only where God is seen does life truly begin. Only when we meet the living God in Christ do we know what life is. We are not some casual and meaningless product of evolution. Each of us is the result of a thought of God. Each of us is willed, each of us is loved, each of us is necessary. There is nothing more beautiful than to be surprised by the Gospel, by the encounter with Christ."[8]

"Seek and Ye Shall Find"

How heaven began to instill the quality of faith in the boy prophet Joseph Smith is of critical importance to this study. Because the foundation principle of the gospel is faith in the Lord Jesus Christ, we would do well to carefully review Joseph's history for clues as to how he learned this essential quality. His maternal grandfather, Solomon Mack, had for decades lived a life far removed from God, but in his declining years he underwent a remarkable conversion to Christ that changed the entire course and direction of his remaining life. In *A Narrative of the Life of Solomon Mack,* published in 1811 when Joseph Smith was only six years old, Solomon Mack bore powerful witness that his faith in Christ had changed the moral compass of his life.[9] "I prayed to the Lord, if he was with me, that I might know it by this token—that my pains might all be eased for that night. And blessed be the Lord, I was entirely free from pain that night. And I rejoiced in the God of my salvation—and found Christ's promises verified. . . . Everything appeared new and beautiful. Oh how I loved my neighbors. How I loved my enemies—I could pray for them. . . . The love of Christ is beautiful. There is more satisfaction to be taken in the enjoyment of Christ one day, than in half a century serving our master, the devil."[10]

How much influence Solomon had on Joseph Smith is not known; however, Joseph was born on the Solomon Mack farm. And because Solomon did not die until the year of the First Vision, it is likely that grandfather and grandson had more than a few interesting encounters.

There is little question that Solomon Mack tried hard to instill faith in his children in his later years, as though in a belated effort to compensate for lost time. His daughter Lucy Mack, who was always religiously inclined, underwent a remarkable conversion of her own when in the fall of 1802 she lay at death's door suffering from a "hectic fever." Covenanting with God "that if he would let me live, I would endeavor to get that religion that would enable me to serve him right, whether it was in the Bible or wherever it might be found," she heard a voice declare, "Seek, and ye shall find; knock, and it shall be opened unto you. Let your heart be comforted." Lucy regained her health and reestablished her covenants and conviction of a personal Savior. Like her father Solomon, she too was never the same afterward and tried hard to instill faith in the Lord Jesus Christ in all her posterity through scripture reading, attending the local Presbyterian church, having personal prayer, and crediting the source of the miracles in her life.[11]

Her husband, Joseph Smith Sr., was prayerful and hardworking, though not an avid churchgoer or member of any particular denomination. He did not "embrace . . . the institutional religion of his time," but he believed in God. If his wife's account is accurate, he was a man prone to visions and dreams. His first came in Royalton, Vermont, in 1811. In one such dream his "guide," or attendant spirit, spoke of a tree in a barren field filled with delicious fruit of which he beckoned his family to come and partake. On the side was a spacious building representing the proud and haughty. Such dreams are reminiscent of Lehi's dream in the Book of Mormon and intimately prepared him to believe in the validity and authenticity of communicating with God in diverse ways.[12]

Joseph's older brothers, Alvin and Hyrum, were also young men of simple faith. In fact, just before Alvin died in 1823, he said to his younger brother: "I want you to be a good boy and do everything that lies in your power to obtain the record [the Book of Mormon]. Be faithful in receiving instruction and in keeping every commandment that is given you."[13]

In addition to learning faith near the fireside of his home, Joseph may likewise have gleaned it from the several preachers of his day and from those who came to hear them and whose lives were changed for good. Near his home in his early teenage years were a great cluster and chorus of competing religions in a revival of Christianity that so convulsed his part of upstate New York that it was long afterward called "The Burned-Over District." Religionists of the various faiths so hotly disagreed on several key points of doctrine that they lost their good feelings for each other in what Joseph later called "a strife of words and a contest about opinions" (Joseph Smith–History 1:6).

Nevertheless, many of his neighbors were men and women of great faith and spiritual conviction, and the lessons the preachers taught of faith in Christ profoundly influenced many and led to an intense spiritual awakening. No doubt some of their lessons and convictions, as well as the spiritual experiences of their listeners, sank deep into Joseph's naturally faith-filled heart as he "attended their several meetings as often as occasion would permit" (Joseph Smith–History 1:8). In his formative years Joseph probably listened to some of the most passionate Bible-based lessons and sermons one could ever hope to hear, and partly because of them, he yearned for the salvation of his soul.

A close examination into the nature of the revivals near Palmyra in 1820 does reveal "a strife of words" and "a contest about opinions" (Joseph Smith–History 1:8); however, not all the revivals were of the circus variety, full of zealous sermonizing, converts barking up trees or baying like dogs, and women swooning in trancelike devotion. Most of the revivals took on the personality and character of the dominant minister. And in the spring of 1820, one such prominent Presbyterian divine was the respected Reverend Asahel Nettleton of Connecticut (assisted by the Reverend Halsey A. Wood), whose travels through the areas west of Albany in late 1819 took the form of a quiet religious reformation.

Preaching in Albany, Schenectady, Saratoga Springs, Ballston, West Galway, Cooperstown, Utica, and rural areas perhaps as far west as Rochester, Nettleton directed his listeners to nearby groves to pray in faith and find hope of salvation. His revivals lasted several weeks and were also characterized by Sabbath sermon meetings in which he taught the awful condition of the fallen and unrepentant soul. These were followed up by "inquiry meetings," "domestic visits," and "family visitations," mainly by devoted women to individual homes for teaching family and individualized prayer, the urgent need to accept Christ as one's personal Savior, and scripture study. The conviction of these religionists was that faith was better instilled by the fireside of the home or cabin than from the pulpit. Thus these revivals took on an intimate, pressing, and personal glow.[14]

In the heart of these revivals—almost always held in the wintertime in such northern climes as New York when fields lay cold and dormant—"anxious meetings" were held almost every night in churches, schools, barns, or any other place large enough to accommodate yearning audiences of anxious sinners seeking salvation. "All the meetings were crowded and solemn. There was no tumult, no noise. Every thing was still, though every mind seemed filled with the magnitude of the work. . . . So profound was the stillness, that a recent death could have added nothing to it, in many families. Common conversation was rarely engaged in, and every ear was open to hear the gospel. . . . The people seemed never weary of attending. . . . They would flock together during all the inclemencies of the season, and listen, when met, with so deep and profound an attention, that in a room crowded to overflowing, it would almost seem you might hear a pin drop or the beating of a watch. The stillness, at times, seemed to have something like mystery about it; it was sublime, it was awful; you almost seemed to be in eternity. . . . Some of the most signal convictions seem to have been wrought by the Spirit in these circumstances."[15]

Nor did the bitter cold of that particular New York winter hold them back. "Our evening meetings [February 1820] were still more thronged, and in the coldest evenings of an unusually severe winter, many assembled who were not able to obtain admittance to our school houses, and have been seen to raise the windows and stand without in devout attention to the word of God."[16]

Wrote another observer of those 1820 upstate New York revivals: "Sometimes, sleigh loads of convinced sinners, after leaving the meeting, and riding half a mile, or a mile, homewards would turn back again to the place of prayer, to hear still more about the salvation of Jesus! And they often did this too, through lanes and ways and snows, that would have been deemed by persons in any other state of mind, to have been impassable."[17] They listened, prayed, and forswore their misdeeds in profound wintry silence, their lives often changed forever in a solemn, dual conviction of sin and guilt on the one hand and a commitment to serve a forgiving Lord and Master on the other.

Such times of "refreshing showers of divine grace" and spiritual "restitution" of preaching, visiting, singing, and covenanting all centered on the faithful reading of scripture. And young Joseph Smith's impressions in reading the Epistle of James were in accord with the design of such revivals. As one contemporary observed, "Generally the first dawning of comfort, in the soul, has been through the application of precious bible truths, while reading the bible, or hearing it explained, or while in the act of secret prayer."[18] The result of such revivals—Presbyterian, Methodist, Baptist, Congregational—was the spiritual conversion of thousands, which usually occurred one at a time in small groups of believers.

Many are the accounts of youth retiring to their own secret groves to pray. Wrote one Reverend Jesse Braman, a Baptist preacher of an 1818–19 revival in Ontario County, near Palmyra: "This part of the wilderness seemed alive for one year. The woods rang with the songs of young converts, and backsliders wept among the trees."[19] Wrote another of the effect of revivals upon the youth in Connecticut in 1817: "Formerly, the children had been accustomed to resort for their juvenile recreations in the hours of play, to a certain grove, in which was a pond of water. Through the whole of last winter they resorted to the same spot; not to engage in youthful sports, but to implore the mercy of Heaven on themselves and their companions."[20]

And young women were as prone to having these experiences as were young men: "One evening towards twilight, a number of young girls, from about eleven to fourteen years of age were very merrily at play on the broad steps of the Baptist meeting house, and of a sudden without visible cause, they were struck with solemn awe, and retired with sighs and sobs, to a house where they spent the evening in reading the Bible, and other good books. Some of these children . . . eventually obtained a comfortable hope, and were baptized."[21]

Thus not only were there many revivals in the region near where Joseph Smith lived in 1820 but the nature of his faithful saga was very much in historical agreement with what others were experiencing, although the results were profoundly different.[22] These wintry revivals were characterized sometimes by argument but also by the "solemnities of eternity," of the Bible being central to conversion and by similarly aged young men and women seeking through faith the salvation of their souls (D&C 43:34). Whatever else one might say about Joseph's accounts, his experience was very much part of the revival culture of his time and place, historically credible and defensible.

"And I Bring Forth My Word unto the Children of Men"

If family, personal experience, revivals, and ministerial sermons contributed to the development of young Joseph's faith, so also did his study of the holy scriptures. The coming forth of the Book of Mormon *and* the faithful preservation and dissemination of the Holy Bible—even to the very threshold of the Smith family farm—were both essential components in the unfolding drama of the Restoration.

With all its flaws, the Bible was the "book of the Lamb of God" promised to come forth unto the remnant of the seed of Israel (1 Nephi 13:38). "And I bring forth my word unto the children of men, yea, even upon all the nations of the earth" (2 Nephi 29:7). The eventual uniting of this "stick of Judah" with the "stick of Joseph" so that they "shall become one in thine hand" (Ezekiel 37:19) could not have happened had not the Bible also come forth. "Wherefore they both shall be established in one" (1 Nephi 13:41).

The rise of the Holy Bible is a miracle in its own right. A modern readership may take for granted the availability of holy writ, but in the early 1800s Bibles were not at all plentiful on the American frontier. In the years immediately leading up to the First Vision, something quite remarkable occurred that went far to create a Bible culture in the West—an awareness and widespread popular ownership of the Bible that had not existed before. The Bible had been printed and been in circulation for centuries, but it was only in the late eighteenth and early nineteenth centuries that it finally began to be printed in vast quantities and distributed worldwide into the hands of millions who previously were too poor to own their own copy.

The spark that ignited the modern Bible movement was a desperate lack of Bibles in northern Wales most poignantly felt by a "sweet Welsh maiden." Since 1791 Wales had been experiencing a religious awakening, and among the converts was a girl about ten years of age named Mary Jones. She walked two miles every Saturday to a relative's home to read from the nearest Bible. Over the next several years, she saved enough money to finally purchase her own. At age seventeen, she walked twenty-eight miles barefoot to buy her first Bible from the Reverend Thomas Charles. As the popular story goes, "He reached her a copy, she paid him the money, and there [they] stood, their hearts too full for utterance, and their tears streaming from their eyes."[23]

Inspired by the young girl's devotion, the Reverend Charles traveled to London in 1802 in quest of ten thousand Welsh Bibles from the almost moribund Society for Promoting Christian Knowledge, an Anglican Bible society that dated from 1698.[24] Its representatives "questioned, doubted, and declined" his request. He then approached the London Missionary Society and the Religious Tract Society. The Reverend Joseph Hughes of the latter group wondered why no vibrant Bible society existed. Subsequently, he and the Reverend Charles, along with William Wilberforce, the Reverend C. Steinkopf, John Owen, and some three hundred others, organized the "Society for Promoting a More Extensive Circulation of the Scriptures at Home and Abroad" in March 1804. Quickly renamed the British and Foreign Bible Society, the fledgling organization immediately garnered interdenominational support. Its purpose was "to encourage a wider dispersion of the Holy Scriptures . . . through the British dominions, and . . . to other countries, whether Christian, Mahomedan, or Pagan."[25] In the space of only three years, the Society printed and distributed 1,816,000 copies of the Bible, testaments, and portions thereof in many different countries and in sixty-six different languages.[26]

Local leaders of various Christian faiths, including some Roman Catholic priests in several areas, began promoting subscriptions, appointing agents, and receiving and filling orders for scriptures. Soon hosts of volunteer "home visitors" and "colporteurs" (traveling salesmen) went from house to house, skirting the traditional bookseller method of distribution. Women served by the thousands at this level, often appointing their own auxiliaries with their own presidents, officers, and appointments. "The Ladies' Associations were enormously more successful and widespread than those of gentlemen."[27] By 1819 the British and Foreign Bible Society counted 629 such auxiliaries, and in 1820 women home visitors in Liverpool alone made 20,800 Bible visits.[28]

And what were the results? By 1834 the British and Foreign Bible Society had distributed 8,549,356 copies in 157 different languages.[29] By 1965, some 723,000,000 volumes had been issued in 829 languages.[30]

In America the need for Bibles was no less real and immediate. Until 1780 almost all Bibles in America had been printed in Great Britain. The Puritans had brought with them the Geneva Bible, first published in 1560, with its notes and teachings by John Calvin. Other immigrants brought the Bishop's Bible, published by the Church of England in 1568.[31] But with the suspension of British imports during the American Revolutionary War, there developed a "famine of Bibles," which was one of the many ills that "a distracted Congress was called upon promptly to remedy."[32]

In 1781 Scottish-born Robert Aitken, at the direction of Congress, became America's first Bible publisher. Isaiah Thomas printed the first folio Bible from an American press ten years later. Quaker Isaac Collins began printing his Bibles, known for their accuracy, that same year. Irish-American Matthew Carey became the best known Bible printer in early America, publishing more than sixty different editions in the early 1800s.[33] Partly because of the Second Great Awakening, the formation of Bible societies, and the aim of evangelizing the West, between 1777 and 1820 four hundred new American editions of the Bible and the New Testament were published.[34] By 1830 that number had climbed to 700.[35]

Yet production could not keep up with population. Between 1790 and 1820 America's population skyrocketed from 3.9 million to 9.6 million, with a large number of Americans not owning their own copies of the Bible. In 1819 the Tennessee Auxiliary Bible Society reported that "the demand is yet great and increasing. The number of the destitute far, very far, surpasses our highest calculations."[36] Even large metropolitan areas such as New York City and Philadelphia were reported as seriously lacking in Bibles.[37]

Such a scarcity had been the reason for the organization of the Philadelphia Bible Society in 1808 and the organization of the Connecticut, Massachusetts, and New York Bible Societies in 1809. Scores of others followed throughout New England and in the South. Finally, in 1816 Elias Boudinot, a former New Jersey delegate to the Continental Congress, presided over the creation of the American Bible Society with forty-two other smaller state and regional societies merged under its expanding banner.[38] By 1820, after just four years in operation, the American Bible Society had printed and distributed 231,552 Bibles and New Testaments.[39] By 1830 the number stood at 1,084,000.[40]

Bibles were similarly scarce on the western New York frontier.

An 1824 Bible society report from Rochester, New York, indicated that in Monroe County alone, near where the Smith family was living, 2,300 families were without Bibles.[41] An 1825 report indicated that at least 20 percent of Ohio families had no Bible, and in thirty-six counties in Alabama, half the citizens did not own scriptures.

Which edition of the Bible ultimately fell into Joseph Smith's hands is not recorded. Considering the indigent circumstances of his home life, it was probably one of the cheaper King James editions and may not have even been his family's own copy. But members of the Smith family were the beneficiaries of many men and women of faith who gave their heart and soul, as it were, to the miraculous distribution of the Bible throughout the Western world in the years leading up to the First Vision.

"But Let Him Ask in Faith"

While wondering what his future course of action should be, Joseph one day turned in the Bible to the Epistle of James, chapter 1, his eyes settling upon these life-changing words: "If any of you lack wisdom, let him ask of God. . . . But let him ask in faith, nothing wavering" (vv. 5–6). Joseph later said that "never did any passage of scripture come with more power to the heart of man than this did at this time to mine." He "reflected on it again and again," finally deciding to "do as James directs, that is, ask of God" (Joseph Smith–History 1:11–13).

President Henry B. Eyring has emphasized that young Joseph's faith to ask of God in prayer "came after pondering a scripture which assured him of God's loving nature. He prayed, as we must, with faith in a loving God. He prayed with the intent not only to listen but to obey. He did not ask only to know the truth. He was committed to act upon whatever God would communicate to him. . . . And because of his faithfulness, in the days and months and years ahead his prayers were answered with a flood of light and truth."[42]

And of Joseph's newfound determination to ask of God, President George Q. Cannon said: "Like a flash of sunlight through lowering clouds, the import of a mighty truth burst upon Joseph's mind. He had been vainly asking help from men who had answered him out of their own darkness. He determined now to seek assistance from God."[43]

Joseph Smith planned to pray as he had never prayed before. "At length," he said, he "came to the determination to 'ask of God'" (Joseph Smith–History 1:13)—to have a vocal communication or dialogue with his Heavenly Father in a predetermined place, in a predetermined fashion, and at a predetermined time. This would be no idle or casual effort but rather the carefully constructed attempt of a searching, faithful young boy to reach the God he earnestly believed in. The precise day is not recorded, although it came early in the spring of 1820—at a time in the northern clime when receding snows may still have been on the ground and on a day when his absence would not have been overly conspicuous. We do know the approximate place, however, and we certainly sense from his writings that it was a carefully planned and premeditated effort.

Yet even with all his preparations, as President Gordon B. Hinckley taught, "it was faith, the simple faith of a fourteen-year-old boy, that took him into the woods that spring morning. It was faith that took him to his knees in pleading for understanding. The marvelous fruit of that faith was a vision glorious and beautiful, of which this great work is but the extended shadow."[44] President Stephen L Richards wrote of Joseph's faith as the great

on a battle royal that threatened his destruction . . . [but] he was protected by the glory of the Lord."[47]

Joseph remembered that he was about to "sink into despair and to abandon [himself] to destruction—not to an imaginary ruin, but to the power of some actual being from the unseen world" (Joseph Smith–History 1:16). What was at stake in this "battle royal" was his very life. At that point his planned, premeditated vocal prayer had become an intensely silent and desperate struggle between life and death. "At this moment of great alarm," his overwhelming concern was probably less about which church he should join than a plea for God's intervention to save him (Joseph Smith–History 1:16).

It has been said there are no atheists in foxholes. Oftentimes we utter our most powerful, *faith-filled* prayers on our way into the operating room or at the bedside of cherished loved ones who are sick or dying. Such critical moments demand our most earnest supplications, for when lives are on the line, our prayers can become so intense that they almost bend the walls. And heaven stoops to listen.

Such was the agonizing situation in which Joseph Smith found himself that spring morning in 1820. Unable to speak and doomed to destruction by the "mystery of iniquity" (2 Thessalonians 2:7), he turned to the very one he had come to address, no longer in the spirit of a merely earnest request but in a desperate, faithful pleading for his life. He was now totally dependent upon that God who had brought him there in the first place: "Exerting all my powers [and faith] to call upon God to deliver me out of the power of this enemy which had seized upon me . . . just at this moment of great alarm, I saw a pillar of light exactly over my head, above the brightness of the sun, which descended gradually until it fell upon me. It no sooner appeared than I found myself delivered from the enemy which held me bound. When the light rested upon me I saw two Personages, whose brightness and glory defy all description, standing above me in the air. One of them spake unto me, calling me by name and said, pointing to the other—*This is My Beloved Son. Hear Him!*" (Joseph Smith–History 1:16–17).

Filled with joy in this moment of divine deliverance, Joseph recalled regaining possession of himself, gratefully realizing that he was still alive and proposing, perhaps almost sheepishly in the awe-inspiring presence of the Divine, the very question that had brought him there: "Which of all the sects was right . . . and which I should join" (Joseph Smith–History 1:18).

In this school of the prophet, young Joseph learned more about the Godhead—the separate identity and reality of God the Father, his Son, Jesus Christ, and the Holy Ghost—than a thousand books or a multitude of religious professors could ever have taught him. He was answered "that I must join none of them, for they were all wrong" (Joseph Smith–History 1:19). He would subsequently learn that he would be instrumental in the hands of God to bring about the Restoration and much righteousness. Christ did not condemn the people for their faith and many excellent works, but he stated categorically that "all their creeds were an abomination" and their "professors were all corrupt" (Joseph Smith–History 1:19).

The structure of the vision—the appearance of both God the Father and Jesus Christ, one in the express image of the other and each possessing glory beyond description—was itself designed so "that faith also might increase in the earth" (D&C 1:21) among those who would later read Joseph's account. President George Q. Cannon taught of the coming of God in the First Vision: "Now, it was meant that this knowledge should be restored first of all. It seems so, at least, from the fact that God Himself came; it seems that this knowledge had to be restored as the basis for all true faith to be built upon. There can be no faith that is not built upon a true conception of God our Father. Therefore, before even angels came, He came Himself accompanied by His Son and revealed Himself once more to man upon the earth."[48]

Yet for our present purposes, the opening of the heavens taught Joseph a remarkable lesson in faith, one that changed his life forever. He learned that the conjunction of his faith with the purposes of God had made his theophany possible. As President Thomas S. Monson once put it, "When Joseph, the boy prophet, went down upon bended knee to seek the help of Almighty God, that God, the Father, and Jesus, the Son, did not appear until after his faith had been tested."[49]

The moment is reminiscent of an ancient Book of Mormon Jaredite prophet who saw not only the finger of God but also his entire person. "Because of thy faith thou hast seen that I shall take upon me flesh and blood; and never has man come before me with such exceeding faith as thou hast. . . . Ye are redeemed from the fall; therefore ye are brought back into my presence; therefore I show myself unto you" (Ether 3:9, 13).

"Their Faith in Their Prayers"

There remains one other venue of faith to explore. Long before Joseph Smith went into the grove near his log cabin home, others centuries earlier had in faith prayed him there. As much as believing Latter-day Saints look upon the First Vision as an event prophesied, foreordained, and predicated upon a young boy's faith, there was another equation of faith at work in the divine mathematics of the Restoration, one that speaks directly to the gospel perspective on history, agency, and divine intervention in the affairs of humankind.

The pattern is that of the binding, encompassing covenants, or promises, of God that stretch across generations of time. When Enoch cried in faith that God might "have mercy upon Noah and his seed, that the earth might never more be covered by the floods. And the Lord could not withhold" and swore unto Enoch "with an oath, that he would stay the floods. . . . And he sent forth an unalterable decree, that a remnant of his seed should always be found among all nations, while the earth should stand" (Moses 7:50–52). Furthermore, Christ's second coming in the last days, as much as it has been prophesied, will occur because of a promise made between God and man. "And the Lord said unto Enoch: As I live, even so will I come in the last days, in the days of wickedness and vengeance, to fulfil the oath which I have made unto you concerning the children of Noah" (Moses 7:60).

The Restoration itself came as a result of ancient covenant. One of the few psalms of the Doctrine and Covenants reads as follows:

> *The Lord hath brought again Zion;*
> *The Lord hath redeemed his people, Israel,*
> *According to the election of grace,*
> *Which was brought to pass by the faith*
> *And covenant of their fathers.* (D&C 84:99)

Such a thing as indispensable as the restoration of the gospel and with it the translation of the Book of Mormon, the coming forth of other scriptures, the gathering of Israel in the latter days from the four corners of the earth, the restoration of priesthood powers and keys, and even Christ's eventual triumphant return—all these things hinged upon more than a young boy's faith. They also depended upon the lives of great men and women of faith who lived long before. Answers to faithful prayers, particularly those of earlier generations, are one of the means by which God involves himself in the affairs of men.

The coming forth of the Book of Mormon, and by extension the calling and preparation of its translator, came in answer to faith. "This work does contain all those parts of my gospel which my holy prophets, yea, and also my disciples, desired in their prayers should come forth unto this people. And I said unto them, that it should be granted unto them according to their faith in their prayers" (D&C 10:46–47). Thus men and women prayed in such faith that God promised to respond. "Yea, and this was their faith—that my gospel, which I gave unto them that they might preach in their days, might come unto their brethren the Lamanites. . . . Now, this is not all—their faith in their prayers was that this gospel should be made known also, if it were possible that other nations should possess this land; and thus they did leave a blessing upon this land in their prayers, that whosoever should believe in this gospel in this land might have eternal life" (D&C 10:48–50).

Even Joseph's specific role as curtain-raiser of the Restoration came because of this covenant of faith. According to the writings of Lehi, "Joseph who was carried captive into Egypt . . . obtained a promise of the Lord" that he would "raise up" a "seer" of Joseph's lineage in the latter days. That seer, named after Joseph, would bring forth "the knowledge of the covenants which I have made with thy fathers." With the calling of this modern "seer" would eventually come the translation, publication, and dissemination of the Book of Mormon (2 Nephi 3:4–7).

And why? "Because of their [the fathers'] faith their words

shall proceed forth out of my mouth unto their brethren who are the fruit of thy loins; and the weakness of their words will I make strong in their faith, unto the remembering of my covenant which I made unto thy fathers." And because of the assurance he had received from the Lord, Joseph said, "Behold, I am sure of the fulfilling of this promise" (2 Nephi 3:21, 14).

Thus Joseph Smith's first prayer was preceded by other faithful prayers of earlier prophets and disciples whom God could not but answer "sometime, somewhere."[50] Faithful man's binding of God is what makes prophecy more certain than history and allows heaven into the picture of what only appears to be divine intervention. "And now, behold, according to their faith in their prayers will I bring this part of my gospel to the knowledge of my people" (D&C 10:52). "And thus by faith, they did lay hold upon every good thing" (Moroni 7:25).

Conclusion

The first principle of the gospel—faith in the Lord Jesus Christ—was abundantly taught in the First Vision of the Restoration to its first student and apprentice prophet. Among so many other glorious truths taught that spring day, this principle will ever remain one of the great legacies of the Sacred Grove. Since so much of the oncoming Restoration would depend upon the young man charged to bring it forth, nothing would be left to chance, especially something so critical as learning the principle of faith in the Lord Jesus Christ. When he returned to the family cabin later that day, he said to his faithful mother, "All is well. . . . I have learned for myself that Presbyterianism is not true" (Joseph Smith–History 1:20).

Joseph Smith had learned more about God the Father and His

Son, Jesus Christ, and their literal dual reality and separate identity than perhaps any other person then alive. He returned from the grove knowing well enough not to join with the ministers of his day. Their faithful yearnings and solemn strivings had found in his vision their finest fulfillment. And Joseph returned home knowing more about himself than we may realize. His faith in Christ, the earnest expectation and fervent hope that demands response, coupled with the faith of prophets long before, had opened the heavens. It was a lesson that would serve him well for the mission with which he was now entrusted.

Chapter Two

THE OFFICE OF THEIR MINISTRY IS TO CALL MEN UNTO REPENTANCE

He that covereth his sins shall
not prosper: but whoso confesseth and forsaketh
them shall have mercy.
PROVERBS 28:13

If faith in the Lord Jesus Christ was the operative first principle of the First Vision, what opened the heavens the second time? The Prophet provides an answer in his own account: "On the evening of the above-mentioned twenty-first of September, after I had retired to my bed for the night, I betook myself to prayer and supplication to Almighty God for forgiveness of all my sins and follies" (Joseph Smith–History 1:29). If the message of the gospel was to be lived by the one entrusted and foreordained to bring it forth, it only stands to reason that he would be inspired to repent and seek help to overcome his weaknesses in order to have purged from him the imperfections in his life.

Joseph Smith was continually instructed in the principles of repentance and forgiveness, but we will emphasize three different periods of time: (1) from 1820, following the First Vision, until he received the plates in September 1827; (2) from September 1827 until the summer of 1828, when Martin Harris lost 116 manuscript pages; and (3) the period of translation from April 1829 until late June 1829, during which time Joseph finished translating the Book of Mormon with Oliver Cowdery acting as his scribe.

Though we must consider Joseph's stumbling blocks, we do so to see how he transformed them into stepping stones. And though it is true that he sinned, as we all do, Joseph became a master at repentance. He learned, as every one of us must, to employ the first principles of the gospel as the instruments for change and improvement, which they are meant to be. And in the process he played a symphony.

"Lay Aside Every Sin"

Repentance is a gift of a loving God. The hallmark of the teachings of Abinadi, Samuel the Lamanite, and John the Baptist, repentance is more than a onetime or even occasional act of dutiful obedience; rather, it is a spirit of humility and contrition that must come to permeate one's character and daily walk. It incorporates an astute sense that despite our best efforts, we sin and fall short of the glory of God.

Said the apostle John, "If we say that we have not sinned, we make him a liar, and his word is not in us" (1 John 1:10). And as King Benjamin put it, "Are we not all beggars? Do we not all depend upon the same Being, even God . . . ?" (Mosiah 4:19). It is only through the atoning blood of Jesus Christ that we have hope for entrance into the kingdom of God.

Elder James E. Talmage taught that the nature of repentance embodies "(1) a conviction of guilt; (2) a desire to be relieved from the hurtful effects of sin; and (3) an earnest determination to forsake sin and to accomplish good."[1] True conviction of sin leads to confession. "For godly sorrow worketh repentance to salvation" (2 Corinthians 7:10). "He that covereth his sins shall not prosper: but whoso confesseth and forsaketh them shall have mercy" (Proverbs 28:13). "By this ye may know if a man repenteth of his sins—behold, he will confess them and forsake them" (D&C 58:43). Such confession, either to the offended party or to ecclesiastical authority—or both, as the case may demand—and heartfelt prayer demonstrate a courageous act of faith and a critical step forward in setting one's feet back on the path of happiness.

Furthermore, the repentant sinner must be willing to forgive others if he or she desires to obtain forgiveness. "I, the Lord, will forgive whom I will forgive, but of you it is required to forgive all men" (D&C 64:10). Is it just to punish others and to harbor ill will and grudges against them when we ourselves are seeking clemency? "Wherefore, I say unto you, that ye ought to forgive one another; for he that forgiveth not his brother his trespasses standeth condemned before the Lord; for there remaineth in him the greater sin" (D&C 64:9). Like a noose around our necks, our refusal to forgive chokes our ability to love.

Repentance has never been popular in a world intent on doing its own thing. It seems particularly unpopular in today's society, which is trying hard to lose the sense of sin. Pope Benedict XVI observed: "Hardly anyone . . . dares nowadays to proclaim the prophetic message: Repent! Hardly anyone dares to make to our age this elementary evangelical appeal." Many sociologists and psychologists see sin as "an illusion or a complex." Likewise, the law seeks to minimize guilt. Even religious education tries hard to evade it. Thus "sin has become a suppressed subject."[2]

Repentance is not a principle of oppressive guilt, nor is it an invitation to continual self-condemnation. These elements often lead to repentance and may even strengthen it, but the spirit of repentance is not a negative one. Essentially it is a positive, uplifting, powerfully liberating spirit of improvement, a constant desire to do better, to love more deeply, to bless others more completely, to live life in all its positive, fruitful aspects to the fullest. It is motivated and accompanied by meekness and humility, neither of which means weakness or self-demeaning, self-destructive behavior. Repentance is a turning away from pride and self-justification, self-satisfaction, and self-fulfillment to an ever-increasing reliance upon Christ and upon the sanctifying power of the Holy Ghost.

Repentance is best motivated by faith, not fear. Nevertheless, it incorporates a clear vision of guilt and an understanding of how deep the abyss of sin really is, how fine the line between real happiness and abject despair is, and how poisonous and destructive sin in all its masquerading and counterfeiting deceptions can be. "He that committeth sin is of the devil; for the devil sinneth from the beginning" (1 John 3:8). Thus repentance encompasses a fear of sin but embraces a love and dependency on God. It is a realization that one cannot win the fight against one's love of sinning alone. True repentance inevitably leads to personal power, liberty, and a wonderful self-reliant dependency on the Lord.

The truth is, faith without repentance is dead. But if faith leads to changing one's life and to a desire to repent in all respects, then that "faith unto repentance" spoken of in scripture leads to baptism and covenants—the making of pledges and committing to put into action a spirit of newness, wanting to do better, and becoming a new creature (Alma 34:15–17). Baptism signifies a new life of trying to keep our covenants with God and become the better person we yearn to be.

We may know that we have truly repented when past sins or weaknesses, once overcome, have become new strengths of character and resolve. They no longer are stumbling blocks but stepping stones. Furthermore, repentance is a revelation in which the obsessive consciousness of one particular sin finally gives way to the awareness of other sins and imperfections perhaps unnoticed before, not in a spirit of discouragement or despair but of quiet confidence and an unwavering willingness to go on unto perfection and "lay aside every . . . sin which doth so easily beset us" (Hebrews 12:1). Repentance, then, is eternal progression in the here and now.

The great irony is that sin, or at least the agonizing sense of our imperfections, may draw us to Christ. Although we no more commit sin to know Christ than we would cut off a limb to know a surgeon, we can and must learn from the error of our ways. Repentance is a wonderful school of the soul, and the penitent heart sets a new course for living.

"That His Sins Were Forgiven"

During the time between his First Vision in the spring of 1820 and September 1823, three and a half years of adolescence, Joseph confesses that he mingled "with all kinds of society" and "frequently fell into many foolish errors, and displayed the weakness of youth" (Joseph Smith–History 1:28). He does not go into detail as to what those errors were, but most of us will readily identify with him. Not only do our sins condemn us but likewise our foolishness, rash judgments, unkind and hasty words, vain imaginations, careless behaviors, and wasting of time and talent. As Nephi warned, "They sell themselves for naught; . . . for the reward of their pride and their foolishness they shall reap destruction" (2 Nephi 26:10). Although Joseph asserts that he was not "guilty of any great or malignant sins," it appears evident that he had a magnified sense of his sins, for he "often felt condemned" for his imperfections and earnestly sought "forgiveness of all [his] sins and follies" (Joseph Smith–History 1:28–29).

It is a true principle that the closer we come to God in prayer and daily behavior, the more God will show us our weaknesses and stumbling blocks. "And if men come unto me I will show unto them their weakness," the Lord told the Book of Mormon prophet Moroni. "I give unto men weakness that they may be humble; and my grace is sufficient for all men that humble themselves before me; for if they humble themselves before me, and have faith in me, then will I make weak things become strong unto them" (Ether 12:27). As is often the case, as we pray for answers to what we consider to be our major problem, God in his wisdom first shows us the beam in our own eye. Although sin is ever destructive, the consciousness of sin can activate the conscience, which as part of the light of Christ can prompt us to turn away and cause us to "forget the thing which is wrong" (D&C 9:9).

So it was with young Joseph Smith. He may have had perfect faith, but he was not a perfect man. What drove him to prayer that night in September 1823 in the family's log cabin near Palmyra was a strong desire for "forgiveness of all my sins and follies, and also for a manifestation to me, that I might know of my state and standing before him; for I had full confidence in obtaining a divine manifestation, as I previously had one" (Joseph Smith–History 1:29).

The coming of the angel Moroni has long been proclaimed as fulfillment of the apostle John's prophecy: "And I saw another angel fly in the midst of heaven, having the everlasting gospel to preach unto them that dwell on the earth, and to every nation, and kindred, and tongue, and people" (Revelation 14:6). Surely that gospel included the teaching of the first principles.

According to the account written by the "second elder" of this dispensation, Oliver Cowdery, one of the first things Joseph remembered the angel Moroni telling him that night was "that his sins were forgiven, and that his prayers were heard."[3] Before the mission of translating the Book of Mormon could begin, the message of forgiveness first had to be communicated (D&C 20:5–8). Thus, if faith in God had opened the heavens the first time, faith unto repentance opened them the second time.[4] This pattern of sacred instruction would be repeated in different times and places throughout the pages of early Church history.[5]

The prophet Mormon, Moroni's father, who had witnessed much sin and corruption in his lifetime, had well taught the principle of repentance and may even have foretold his own son's ongoing mission: "Neither have angels ceased to minister unto the children of men. For behold, they are subject unto him, to minister according to the word of his command, showing themselves unto them of strong faith and a firm mind in every form of godliness. And the office of their ministry is to call men unto repentance, and to fulfil and to do the work of the covenants of the Father, which he hath made unto the children of men, to prepare the way among the children of men, by declaring the word of Christ unto the chosen vessels of the Lord, that they may bear testimony of him" (Moroni 7:29–31). Angels, therefore, come not to satisfy idle curiosity but to call "chosen vessels" of "strong faith and a firm mind" unto repentance and to fulfill the covenants of God to former generations. And so it was with Joseph Smith that September night in 1823.

While it is entirely appropriate to study Moroni's message in the light of preparing Joseph for his upcoming mission to translate a book that contained "the fulness of the everlasting Gospel" (Joseph Smith–History 1:34), the unfolding scenes and heavenly manifestations of the Restoration also taught the prophet of the

Restoration the first principles of the gospel. Seen from this perspective, some of what Moroni, a master prophet, taught Joseph, an apprentice prophet, may take on added meaning.

The very first scripture quoted by the angel Moroni, although he was a Book of Mormon prophet, came from the Bible—Malachi's warning in the Old Testament against sinning: "For behold, the day cometh that shall burn as an oven, and all the proud, yea, and all that do wickedly shall burn as stubble" (Joseph Smith–History 1:37; see also Malachi 4:1). Then, quoting from the third chapter of Acts in the New Testament, Moroni spoke of Christ, warning the world that "'they who would not hear his voice should be cut off from among the people'" (Joseph Smith–History 1:40; see also Acts 3:22–23). He went on to quote from the second chapter of the book of Joel, including the promise "that whosoever shall call on the name of the Lord"—as Joseph himself had done—"shall be delivered," for surely "your young men shall see visions" (Joel 2:32, 28). Moroni quoted "many other passages of scripture, and offered many explanations" that are not recorded there (Joseph Smith–History 1:41; see also vv. 36–40).

With each of his ensuing nocturnal visits, Moroni repeated everything he had said the first time and then added warnings and information. Little wonder Joseph Smith later recalled that Moroni cited a particular biblical passage "with a little variation from the way it reads in our Bibles" (as was the case with chapter 4 of Malachi) or other passages "precisely as they stand in our New Testament," as was the case of Moroni's citation from Acts (Joseph Smith–History 1:36, 40).

One might see here not only Joseph Smith's commission to translate the Book of Mormon but also, upon completing that work, the invitation to revise the sacred Holy Bible, not to condemn it but to raise and reclaim it. In citing the Bible, the angel

Moroni was proclaiming and redeeming it. Just as the Bible had brought Joseph to the Sacred Grove, so it was here again being used to instruct him in his new mission.

In those first twenty-four hours of instruction, the angel visited Joseph five times—three visitations that took up virtually the entire night, one the next morning while he attempted to climb the fence out of his father's field, and then again at the Hill Cumorah. Warned the night before about getting the gold plates in order to get rich, especially considering the indigent circumstances of his family, Joseph was reprimanded when he made an attempt "to take them out." The angel told him "that the time for bringing them forth had not yet arrived, neither would it, until four years from that time" (Joseph Smith–History 1:53).[6]

We see in this experience the beginning of a course of training and careful instruction that had everything to do with the preparation and establishment of a prophet. As a seventeen-year-old young man in the fall of 1823, Joseph was obviously not ready to receive the plates and with them the mission of translation; nor would he be ready for some time to come. Moroni informed Joseph that on the anniversary of this visit at the hill, he desired to meet with Joseph annually at the same location "until the time should come for obtaining the plates" (Joseph Smith–History 1:53).

The mental, emotional, and spiritual significance of an annual visit with a heavenly being and its potential effect on personal behavior can hardly be overestimated. Charles Dickens recognized this fact in his classic novel *A Christmas Carol.* Ebenezer Scrooge's all-night visits with the spirits changed his life forever. Similarly, Latter-day Saints can identify with the current practice of an annual tithing settlement with their bishop or branch president or with worthiness interviews for temple recommends. There is a wonderful element of covenant accountability in such interviews.

They serve as an opportunity for confessing sins, for repledging souls, and for reestablishing priorities to help us conform with the better good within us. And confession is good for the soul, provided it is not the casual, mental exercise of pretending over our sins but rather the courageous act of admitting them to a sympathetic servant of God. A bishop, though not the source of forgiveness, is yet the agent of divine reconciliation. The scripture says, "By this ye may know if a man repenteth of his sins—behold, he will confess them and forsake them" (D&C 58:43). President George Q. Cannon phrased it this way: "Each time, the messenger visited him on that consecrated spot; chastening him to patience, exacting anew a covenant of self-sacrificing fidelity to the trust, and extending the counsels and instructions pertaining to the re-establishment, at the proper hour, of the Church of Christ upon the earth."[7]

We begin to see in Moroni's curriculum of instruction his role not only as mentor and tutor but also as prophet and bishop. Where was Joseph, having been told to join no existing church, to turn for religious training and edification? His mother, Lucy Mack Smith, and some other members of the family continued to attend the Presbyterian Church, and it is likely that Joseph attended with them on occasion. He obviously held several conversations with ministers during these years and may have told more about his experiences than discretion would have dictated. His father, who had been uniquely prepared to believe in his son's spiritual development through several visions and dreams of his own, believed in the angel's visit and encouraged Joseph, replying "that it was of God" (Joseph Smith–History 1:50). Thus young Joseph likely looked forward to this annual interview as a sacred time to commune, confess, explore, and inquire. The knowledge that such interviews were pending may have wrought enormous impact on his faith, personal behavior, and developing sense of accountability and mission.

There is ample scriptural precedent and pattern for such training. Even though Christ at the tender age of twelve confounded the master teachers of his time, his own mission would not formally begin until he too was much older. In the meantime he continued to receive instruction and preparation, "grace for grace," from his earthly parents and from his Father in Heaven, "until he received a fulness" (D&C 93:12–13) after the Resurrection. During this time, "Jesus increased in wisdom and stature, and in favour with God and man" (Luke 2:52).

The ancient Israelite prophet Samuel was similarly instructed. The Lord had appeared to him when he was a trusting, believing, young boy and likewise had commissioned him, saying, "Behold, I will do a thing in Israel, at which both the ears of every one that heareth it shall tingle." The Lord then took him under his wing of preparation. "Samuel grew, and the Lord was with him, and did let none of his words fall to the ground. And all Israel from Dan even to Beer-sheba knew that Samuel was established to be a prophet of the Lord." Nor did the Lord appear only once to Samuel, for he appeared unto him again in Shiloh, teaching and revealing much to his young prophet (see 1 Samuel 3:9–21).

Mormon writes that when he was only fifteen years of age, yet "being somewhat of a sober mind, therefore I was visited of the Lord, and tasted and knew of the goodness of Jesus" (Mormon 1:15).

Nephi was also prepared by the Lord and by repeated visits from angels of God during his missions of obtaining the plates of Laban and of seeking a new promised land—a course of tutoring his older, rebellious brothers refused to accept.

Joseph Smith does not explain the confidences and confessions he may have expressed during his annual visits with Moroni. Between 1823 and 1827, when Joseph advanced in age from seventeen to twenty-one, he became involved in treasure digging with Josiah Stowell of South Bainbridge (now Afton), New York. Much has been made of Joseph Smith's late 1825 silver mine diggings as a way to supplement his family's meager existence.[8] Though treasure seeking had been a common endeavor in New England and New York for decades and had involved the energies of many, Joseph grew increasingly uncomfortable with the whole process. "I continued to work for nearly a month," he later recorded, "without success in our undertaking, and finally I prevailed with the old gentleman to cease digging after it."[9] He sought to distance himself from the magic culture and folklore associated with it and from the speculative, money-seeking nature of those involved, perhaps having said at times more about angels and gold plates than perhaps he should have. He came to regret his involvement in such activities, and as the time neared to receive the plates, he moved on.

If Joseph chose not to record private matters from his interviews with the angel, he does give us surprising clues and insights into what they did discuss. "Accordingly, as I had been commanded, I went at the end of each year, and at each time I found the same messenger there, and received instruction and intelligence from him at each of our interviews, respecting what the Lord was going to do, and how and in what manner his kingdom was to be conducted in the last days" (Joseph Smith–History 1:54).

One may wonder at the deliberate choice of the words *instruction* and *intelligence*. The former most can comprehend; the latter may have reference to light and truth that only revelation can impart, the kind of heavenly instruction, education, and refinement that sanctify the spirit while instructing the soul. Had Joseph been living a life seriously out of harmony with the commandments of God, it is unlikely he could have received such intelligence.

There was also more to the angel's training sessions than the plates and how to obtain them. He clearly foretold impending events "respecting what the Lord was going to do," events that may have included the process of translation, the restoration of requisite authority, and further angelic instruction. Beyond the near future, Moroni also taught Joseph "how and in what manner his kingdom was to be conducted in the last days" (Joseph Smith–History 1:54). In these annual personal priesthood interviews, is it possible that the Prophet Joseph Smith learned how and when to establish and organize the Church of Jesus Christ and about priesthood offices, temple worship, and much more?

"At length," Joseph Smith received the plates, the Urim and Thummim, and the breastplate on 22 September 1827 from "the same heavenly messenger," with the charge "that I should be responsible for them; that if I should let them go carelessly, or through any neglect of mine, I should be cut off" (Joseph Smith–History 1:59). But if he remained faithful, Joseph would be protected in his work. After four years of prophetic preparation in the principles of truth and righteousness, he was deemed ready and worthy for the next level of instruction. Yet even after all this, he had much yet to learn about repentance.

"I Have Sinned"

To what extent Joseph Smith had confided in others about his visits with the angel Moroni is unknown. Before Joseph received the plates, however, Martin Harris, a well-known farmer and respected citizen of Palmyra, had taken an interest in the young man's emerging mission. Joseph's senior by twenty-two years,

Martin had served as a road commissioner and on several local juries. A committed churchgoer, he had earned a reputation as a student of the Bible. Much of what is known of Harris in these early years we owe to Joseph Smith's own account and to Joseph's mother, whose *History of the Prophet Joseph Smith by His Mother* still stands as an indispensable source, particularly for these formative years. According to her, Martin's marriage to his cousin, Lucy Harris, was less than ideal. Short-tempered and hard of hearing, Lucy strenuously objected to her husband's interest in the budding Palmyra Prophet. She believed it would all lead to no good financially and insisted that she be involved in any of Martin's dealings with the Smith family. Martin's anxiety to substantiate the plausibility, if not the authenticity, of Joseph Smith's work may be perfectly understandable, considering his difficult home situation. After all, it was the Harrises' money and marriage that were on the line.[10]

According to Joseph Smith's own history, well before he had received the plates, "rumor with her thousand tongues" was circulating all about Palmyra, tending to discredit the reputation of the Smith family. The resultant persecution became "so intolerable" that Joseph and Emma decided to move to her parents' home in Harmony, Pennsylvania, some one hundred fifty miles to the south. "In the midst of our afflictions we found a friend in a gentleman by the name of Martin Harris," Joseph recorded, "who came to us and gave me fifty dollars to assist us on our journey" (Joseph Smith–History 1:61). By means of such timely assistance, equal to approximately twenty-five hundred dollars today, the pair left Palmyra and moved to Harmony in December 1827.

Over the next few months, Joseph continued working on the translation of the large plates of Nephi. Between 12 April and 14 June 1828, he and Martin Harris completed 116 foolscap-size pages of transcription with Martin working as scribe. Beset by continuing criticism at home, and perhaps bothered by lingering doubts of his own, Martin then pleaded for Joseph to let him take the completed pages to show his insistent wife and her doubtful family. Unwilling to take no for an answer, Joseph asked again. When the Lord consented to Joseph's third request, Joseph eventually surrendered the manuscript to his friend and benefactor. Regrettably, he did not make a copy.

Martin returned to Palmyra, where the worst of his intentions got the best of him. Carelessly breaking his promise to show the pages only to his wife, a selected few family members, and a "very particular friend,"[11] he proved an unfaithful guardian of the sacred text. Before long he had lost it, perhaps having lent the pages to others.

Meanwhile, hearing no news from Martin—which, in Lucy Mack Smith's words, "was altogether aside of the arrangement when they separated"—Joseph faced intensified worries that same spring of 1828 while confronting another crisis at home. Emma had given birth to their first child, a son, who died shortly thereafter. Remaining at his wife's bedside day and night for two weeks during her difficult recovery, Joseph worried not only about her health but also about the state and condition of the manuscript. Finally, at Emma's urging, he went to Palmyra to learn the cause of Martin's silence.[12]

The morning of the intended rendezvous, Martin was late for breakfast at the Smith home by six hours, evidently stalling and searching, while Joseph and the rest of the family impatiently fretted within. Finally they saw him coming along the lane with a slow, measured gait, his eyes fixed upon the ground. When he reached the fence, he got up on it and drew his hat over his eyes.

At length he entered the house. Lucy records what happened next:

"Martin took up his knife and fork as if to use them but dropped them from his hands. Hyrum said, 'Martin, why do you not eat? Are you sick?' Martin pressed his hands upon his temples and cried out in a tone of anguish, 'Oh! I have lost my soul. I have lost my soul.'

"Joseph, who had smothered his fears till now, sprang from the table, exclaiming, 'Oh! Martin, have you lost that manuscript? Have you broken your oath and brought down condemnation upon my head as well as your own?'

"'Yes,' replied Martin, 'it is gone, and I know not where.'

"'Oh, my God, my God,' said Joseph, clinching his hands together. 'All is lost, is lost! What shall I do? I have sinned. It is I who tempted the wrath of God by asking him for that which I had no right to ask, as I was differently instructed by the angel. . . . Then must I,' said Joseph, 'return to my wife with such a tale as this? I dare not do it lest I should kill her at once. And how shall I appear before the Lord? Of what rebuke am I not worthy from the angel of the Most High?'"[13]

In this moment of awful anguish we glimpse something of the character of Joseph Smith and the extent to which he had been taught. A lesser man would likely have turned on Martin Harris and soundly berated him for his mistaken judgment. Human nature often blames someone else for causing problems, especially when that someone else shares much of the fault. But in that heated moment of despair, Joseph rose to his calling, taking full responsibility for the entire matter. "I have sinned. It is I who tempted the wrath of God," he said. If the first step of repentance is accepting one's own accountability and responsibility, Joseph was the troubled teacher and Martin his tormented student.

Lucy goes on to describe the depth of remorse her son showed. "I besought him not to mourn so," she said, hoping to offer some sort of consolation, "for it might be that the Lord would forgive him, after a short season of humiliation and repentance on his part. But what could I say to comfort him when he saw all the family in the same state of mind that he was? Our sobs and groans and the most bitter lamentations filled the house. Joseph, in particular, was more distressed than the rest, for he knew definitely and by sorrowful experience the consequence of what would seem to others to be a very trifling neglect of duty. He continued walking backwards and forwards, weeping and grieving like a tender infant until about sunset, when we persuaded him to take a little nourishment."[14]

Leaving for Harmony immediately after this episode, Joseph continued prayerful, sensing a pending day of reckoning. Subsequently the angel Moroni once again appeared to him, soundly censuring him for having delivered the manuscript into the hands of "a wicked man" (D&C 3:12). Joseph said, "As I had ventured to become responsible for this man's faithfulness, I would of necessity suffer the consequences of his indiscretion, and I must now give back the Urim and Thummim into his (the angel's) hands."[15]

The revelation Joseph received that summer of 1828 chastised him in no uncertain terms. In disarmingly frank and self-condemning terms, he recorded these words of divine rebuke:

"Behold, how oft you have transgressed the commandments and the laws of God, and have gone on in the persuasions of men. For, behold, you should not have feared man more than God. Although men set at naught the counsels of God, and despise his words—Yet you should have been faithful; and he would have extended his arm and supported you against all the fiery darts of the adversary; and he would have been with you in every time of trouble. . . . For thou hast suffered the counsel of thy director to be trampled upon from the beginning" (D&C 3:6–8, 15).

In this reprimand, Joseph was severely scolded for what seems to have been a series of past sins and repeated foolish acts that, had they persisted, might well have disqualified him from his work. Whether one interprets the term "thy director" to be the angel Moroni, this much is clear: Joseph had carelessly sinned or fallen short on several occasions and had made some poor choices. Of Joseph's chastisement and subsequent remorse, President George Q. Cannon wrote: "The sorrow and humiliation which Joseph felt were beyond description. The Lord's rebukes for his conduct pierced him to the center. He humbled himself in prayer and repentance; and so true was his humility that the Lord accepted it as expiation."[16] Joseph lost his privileges of translation "for a season," a time of probation during which he continued to learn humility and penitence, becoming more aware that the restoration of the gospel and the translation of the Book of Mormon would come to pass with or without him and only upon the principles of righteousness.

Some might wonder at the strictness of the Lord in chastening and reprimanding his prophet and in describing Martin Harris, who was trying to help, as "a wicked man" (D&C 3:12). Perhaps this episode sheds light on the designs of God, whose ways are higher than our ways and whose thoughts are higher than our thoughts (Isaiah 55:9). God neither is the author of sin nor causes it for his purposes. As James indicates, "Let no man say when he is tempted, I am tempted of God: for God cannot be tempted with evil, neither tempteth he any man" (James 1:13). "For I the Lord cannot look upon sin with the least degree of allowance; nevertheless, he that repents and does the commandments of the Lord shall be forgiven" (D&C 1:31–32). Those who are forgiven are restored to their place and mission in life. If this is true of the common man, how much more so a prophet of God? Nevertheless, "as many as I love, I rebuke and chasten" (Revelation 3:19), and "whom the Lord loveth he chasteneth . . . that we might be partakers of his holiness" (Hebrews 12:6, 10).

This same principle of purity and holiness is well taught in the very book Joseph was about to translate. Nephi the son of Nephi, who became Christ's chief disciple in ancient America, wrote that "there was not any man who could do a miracle in the name of Jesus save he were cleansed every whit from his iniquity" (3 Nephi 8:1). Could a miracle as great as the translation of the Book of Mormon have come to pass in any other way? Surely a book so steeped in the doctrine of repentance and forgiveness could not have come forth without the willing and active repentance of the one charged to bring it forth.

Happily for Joseph, three months later, on 22 September 1828, the fifth anniversary of the angel's first appearance, the Prophet experienced the fruits of his penitence. "I had the joy and satisfaction of again receiving the Urim and Thummim," he said. His angelic mentor also "was rejoiced" at the lessons Joseph had learned in repentance and "told me that the Lord was pleased with my faithfulness and humility, and loved me for my penitence and diligence in prayer."[17]

The story of Joseph Smith, Moroni, Martin Harris, and the lost manuscript has one concluding episode. Nine months later near the end of June 1829 at the farm of Peter Whitmer Sr. in Fayette, New York, the same angel Moroni appeared to the Three Witnesses—Martin Harris, David Whitmer, and Oliver Cowdery. Just as Moroni had come to Joseph Smith in September 1823 to declare forgiveness and to teach him the principles of repentance and forgiveness, so also his visit to Martin was predicated upon that same saving principle. When indicating to Martin the possibility that he might be one of the Three Witnesses, Joseph said, "Martin Harris . . . *you* have got to humble yourself before your God this day and obtain, if possible, a forgiveness of your sins. If you will do this, it is God's will that you . . . should look upon the plates."[18] Well-known in Church history is the fact that after Martin, David, and Oliver retired to the woods near the Whitmer home, nothing happened until Martin excused himself, believing, "as he expressed himself, that his presence was the cause of our not obtaining what we wished for. He accordingly withdrew," and the angel appeared to Joseph and the other two men. Only after Joseph rejoined Martin and accompanied him in fervent prayer was the same vision opened to his view. "''Tis enough; 'tis enough,' he cried; 'mine eyes have beheld; mine eyes have beheld;' and jumping up, he shouted, 'Hosanna,' blessing God, and otherwise rejoiced exceedingly."[19] Like Joseph, Martin also had to learn the first principles.

Joseph Smith, Oliver Cowdery, and the Process of Translation, 1829

We now come to our third and final episode, that period of translation in which Joseph Smith and his new scribe, Oliver Cowdery, completed the Book of Mormon. Of virtually the same age as Joseph, Oliver (1806–50) was also from Vermont, had been a store clerk, and had taught in country schools. While boarding with Joseph's parents, he had learned of the ancient record and the lost 116 pages. What piqued his interest in the work was that he had "inquired of the Lord" about the matter. As recorded in the Doctrine and Covenants, "as often as thou hast inquired thou hast received instruction of my Spirit. If it had not been so, thou wouldst not have come to the place where thou art at this time"

(D&C 6:14). The Prophet's first history explains that the "Lord appeared unto . . . Oliver Cowdery and shewed unto him the plates in a vision and . . . what the Lord was about to do through me, his unworthy servant. Therefore he was desirous to come and write for me to translate."[20]

The two men met each other on 5 April 1829, became fast friends, arranged some temporal business together the following day, and began the work of translation on 7 April. Though they were partners in the translating process, a great difference between the two men was in their spiritual preparation and in their approach to the task at hand. A teacher by profession who knew how to read, write, and do numbers better than his partner, Oliver was nevertheless Joseph's pupil in the first principles of the gospel.

The profound intellectual challenges Joseph faced in translating an ancient unknown language, even with the aid of the Urim and Thummim, are hinted at in Oliver's parallel but failed experience as a translator. Those difficulties afford us yet another view of how repentance was once more taught during the translation process. Though it is not well-known, the second elder of the Restoration began his mission with the gift to translate. "Ask that you may know the mysteries of God, and that you may translate and receive knowledge from all those ancient records which have been hid up, that are sacred; and according to your faith shall it be done unto you" (D&C 8:11). Nevertheless, as Elder Dallin H. Oaks has indicated, Oliver soon "failed in his efforts to translate."[21] Why? "Behold, it is because that you did not continue as you commenced" (D&C 9:5).

At issue here was more than Oliver's humility or willingness to be taught; also at issue was his aptitude for intellectual application, which was not yet developed enough to bear results—at least not in the timely way then required. Oliver failed in the intellectually demanding work of translating because he had not thoroughly applied himself mentally to the task. Nor, apparently, had he adequately prepared himself spiritually. "Behold, you have not understood; you have supposed that I would give it unto you, when you took no thought save it was to ask me," the Lord told him. "But behold, I say unto you, that you must study it out in your mind; then you must ask me if it be right, and if it is right I will cause that your bosom shall burn within you; therefore, ye shall feel that it is right" (D&C 9:7–8).

Joseph Smith had learned both lessons—mental and spiritual—from his previous experiences. He had been schooled in matters of character and spirit over the previous nine years, and his recent experience with Martin Harris and the loss of the 116 pages was, in hindsight, a preparatory school of remarkable learning. Can we really expect Oliver to have learned the same lessons as well after but a few days at the task?[22]

The intellectual demands of translating were rigorous and extremely challenging. If the experiences and testimony of the Three Witnesses are to be taken at face value, the successful translation of the Book of Mormon was neither magical nor mythical but measured and marvelous, a careful confluence of obedience, recurring repentance, and consequent revelation on the one hand and a rigorous mental exercise of intense study, recall and recognition, and trial and error on the other.

The specifics of translation remain a mystery, but it may be instructive to compare the work of Joseph Smith to his magnificent contemporary and superlative translator of ancient Egyptian hieroglyphic writing, the brilliant French linguist Jean-Francois Champollion. Just five years before, Champollion had finally decoded the mysterious hieroglyphics of the famed Rosetta Stone found near Alexandria by Napoleon's Egyptian army in 1799. After a lifetime of studying Coptic, Arabic, Hebrew, Greek, Egyptian, and a dozen other languages, Champollion, in his famous "Lettre á Monsieur Dacier" of 22 September 1822 (exactly one year before Moroni showed Joseph the plates for the first time), convinced the waiting world that he could read the ancient hieroglyphic writings of Egypt. As a result, "the man from Grenoble" is still rightfully revered as the father of modern Egyptology.

Whereas Champollion naïvely believed at first that a thorough knowledge of Coptic would allow him to directly decipher ancient Egyptian writing symbols, he gradually came to realize that such was quite dauntingly not the case. Hieroglyphic writings were not a single alphabet; they had a wide variety of spellings for the same person or place and featured no vowels but plenty of shorthand contractions, such as, in English, *pkg* for "parking" or *trnsltn* for "translation." Furthermore the ancient Egyptian scribes assumed the reader was conversant with their combinations of right vowels and contractions, "but this knowledge has been lost, although Coptic gives clues to it."[23]

After long and painstaking effort, Champollion concluded that hieroglyphs could not be read alone but rather in groups or clusters. Intently comparing the Greek to the Coptic, the Coptic to a later simplified form of ancient Egyptian writing (demotic), and by extension, the demotic to the hieroglyphic, Champollion noted that there were three times as many hieroglyphic signs as there were Greek words. Therefore there had to be a combination or grouping of signs to convey a single meaning—in other words, consonants and syllables, essential components to phonetic expressions. Though the hieroglyphs employed no vowels, they were a combination of phonetics and pictures. Unlike his scientific contemporaries, such as Thomas Young of England, Champollion was now looking not just for more clues between the hieroglyphic and the demotic but also for the ability to read the maze of what constituted hieroglyphic writing.

What finally enabled Champollion to do what no one else had been able to accomplish was the application of his mastery of Coptic to the problem. As one leading scholar has written, "His knowledge of Coptic enabled him to deduce the phonetic values of many syllabic signs, and to assign correct readings to many pictorial characters, the meanings of which were made known to him by the Greek text on the Stone."[24] The system of decipherment that Champollion had been methodically developing over several years and that was eventually verified was that hieroglyphic script was mainly phonetic but not entirely so; it also contained logograms, or a set of shorthand symbols, used to write names and common nouns from the Pharaonic period. The combination of both constituted an ancient alphabet that Champollion could prove and sufficiently read or decipher. He thus came to the right conclusion that the hieroglyphic writings were not just of the later periods of Egyptian history but of the very earliest Pharaonic era as well. He therefore decoded the entire system and showed that hieroglyphic, hieratic, and demotic all corresponded to the same language. Whereas Thomas Young may well have discovered parts of the alphabet, it was "Champollion [who] unlocked an entire language."[25]

Joseph Smith, on the other hand, could barely read and write one language—English.[26] He had neither the scholarly training nor the linguistic knowledge to decode one symbol after another. Indeed, his mission was not to master the linguistics required to read an ancient language but to translate or convey their meanings into English. His initial work of translation consisted of copying the various "characters," letters, phrases, or hieroglyphs found on the large plates of Nephi into some sort of working alphabet. "I copied a considerable number of them," he records, clear evidence of the strong mental exercise and careful study he too would need before translating could actually begin (Joseph Smith–History 1:62). Then only gradually did he begin to use what neither Champollion nor any other translator had at his command—the "interpreters," or Urim and Thummim (Mosiah 8:13). With the aid of this remarkable ancient instrument, Joseph Smith began to translate some of the characters.

It would appear that the process was less one of decoding or deciphering the precise meaning of the individual characters and inscriptions found on the plates, as Champollion had so painstakingly done with the Rosetta Stone, and more one of discerning the meanings conveyed thereon and then, in addition, transforming such meanings into acceptable King James Bible literary English. Consequently, the interpreters seem to have functioned on two levels: conveying meaning from the ancient text while simultaneously suggesting wording in biblical-sounding English beyond Joseph's limited ability at the time. Thus it would appear that Joseph Smith was not a decoder of ancient signs and symbols or a translator in the Champollion sense but rather a transmitter, translator, and writer who, with the aid of the interpreters, transcribed what he saw into exquisite English prose and poetry.

Oliver was ill-prepared for all of this. The customized reprimand and gentle reproof he received in section 9 of the Doctrine and Covenants was less a rebuke and more a reminder that God had already called and prepared his prophet; what was needed now was a humble, penitent scribe who could serve as a devoted supporter and trusted eyewitness to visions soon to occur. "Do not murmur, my son, for it is wisdom in me that I have dealt with you after this manner. . . . It is not expedient that you should translate now. Behold, it was expedient when you commenced; but you feared, and the time is past, and it is not expedient now; for, do you not behold that I have given unto my servant Joseph sufficient strength, whereby it is made up? And neither of you have I condemned. . . . Be faithful, and yield to no temptation" (D&C 9:6, 10–13). It was a lesson in repentance not missed by either man.

If Joseph and Oliver learned repentance at the outset of translating, they were repeatedly reminded of its central importance as their work progressed. David Whitmer's 1882 remembrance of a time Joseph Smith could not translate, despite all the gifts he had at his command, is well-known.

"He could not translate unless he was humble and possessed the right feelings towards everyone," Whitmer recalled. "To illustrate so you can see. One morning when he was getting ready to continue the translation, something went wrong about the house and he was put out about it. Something that Emma . . . had done. Oliver and I went upstairs [obviously this was at the Whitmer home] and Joseph came up soon after to continue the translation, but he could not do anything. He could not translate a single syllable. He went downstairs, out into the orchard, and made supplication to the Lord; was gone about an hour—came back to the house, and asked Emma's forgiveness and then came up stairs where we were and then the translation went on all right. He could do nothing save he was humble and faithful."[27] To borrow Elder B. H. Roberts's phraseology, the translation "was not merely a mechanical process" but a laboratory of spiritual and mental application governed by the principles found in the book they were now translating.[28] Even after almost ten years of preparation, Joseph Smith relearned the lesson that even the smallest sins or senseless hurts prevented the free flow of inspiration and revelation. By faith, a "faith unto repentance" (Alma 34:15) that led, in turn, to the guiding and revealing influence of the Spirit of the Lord, he lived and obeyed his way through to the end of the translation process.

Conclusion

The foregoing discussion has argued for a new and different perspective from that offered by some of Joseph Smith's biographers. Nowhere have we argued that Joseph was a perfect man without blemish. His sins and imperfections were real, and while we have not dwelt upon them in any way to discredit his reputation, they surely caused him a great deal of grief and hardship. Yet our theme has been that if God called a prophet, he prepared that prophet in the first principles of the gospel.

To repeat, the mission of Moroni in preparing the way for the translation of the Book of Mormon was the charge given to all angelic visitors: "to minister according to the word of his command, showing themselves unto them of strong faith and a firm mind in every form of godliness. And the office of their ministry is to call men unto repentance, and to fulfill and to do the work of the covenants of the Father" (Moroni 7:30–31). Time after time, Moroni, the master prophet, trained Joseph Smith, the apprentice prophet, in matters of the soul, in honesty and integrity, in humility and patience, in repentance and forgiveness.

Joseph Smith's partners in translation, Martin Harris and Oliver Cowdery, were likewise taught the same principles and learned from hard experience that the message of the gospel had to be lived by the messengers of the gospel to have any lasting effect. Integrity, not hypocrisy, would attract the best of men and women and make for a lasting movement. This injunction was repeated all the way up to Fayette and the organization of the Church in April 1830 and for years afterward. "Preach naught but repentance," and "the thing which will be of the most worth unto you will be to declare repentance unto this people, that you may bring souls unto me, that you may rest with them in the kingdom of my Father" (D&C 19:21; 15:6; 16:6).

Indeed, these lessons of repentance and forgiveness would be repeated numerous times throughout the pages of Church history, including the vision in the Kirtland Temple in April 1836: "Behold, your sins are forgiven you; you are clean before me; therefore, lift up your heads and rejoice" (D&C 110:5).

Chapter Three

I KNOW THE DOOR: BAPTISM BY IMMERSION FOR THE REMISSION OF SINS

And he commandeth all men that they must repent, and be baptized in his name, having perfect faith in the Holy One of Israel.

2 Nephi 9:23

Just before his ascension, the resurrected Christ prophesied to his apostles that after they received the Holy Ghost they would become "witnesses unto me both in Jerusalem, and in all Judaea, and in Samaria, and unto the *uttermost part* of the earth" (Acts 1:8; emphasis added). Was it possible that such a prophecy extended as far afield as the Americas and as far into the future as modern times?

The Susquehanna River is one of the longest rivers on the American East Coast. Draining more than twenty-seven thousand square miles of the rural heartland of Pennsylvania, New York, and Maryland, the two main branches of the Susquehanna combine near Northumberland, Pennsylvania, and eventually empty into the upper Chesapeake Bay. Anciently the Susquehannock, an Iroquoian Indian tribe, lived along the banks of the river and gave the Susquehanna its name, signifying "mile wide, foot deep"—referring to the river's characteristically slow, shallow, and muddy current. Soon after the Revolutionary War, the river became an important transportation corridor with the discovery of vast coal deposits in the Appalachian Mountains. But with such shallow rapids, the Susquehanna begged for the construction of a system of dams and canals to allow for the transportation of coal, lumber, produce, and increasing passenger traffic.

When Isaac Hale, Emma Smith's father, who had been born in Connecticut, moved upriver to settle near Harmony, Pennsylvania, in 1790, the commercial development of the river was in its infancy. Called "Nimrod" by his pioneering neighbors for his reputation as a hunter, Isaac, along with his wife, Elizabeth, were early and well-respected settlers in the region. Together they raised a family of nine children, the seventh being Emma Hale, born 10 July 1804. As a child she loved to ride horses and to canoe on the Susquehanna with her brothers. Tall, gangly, and better educated than most of her siblings, Emma grew to be a pretty, dark-haired woman.

Although it never became a major commercial waterway because of its rapids and shallows, the Susquehanna River, even in the time of Isaac and Elizabeth Hale, was becoming a popular thoroughfare for tourists eager to visit the already famous Niagara Falls. In these pre-Erie Canal days, the Susquehanna formed an essential link in the favored waterway route extending north from Chesapeake Bay to Harrisburg and on up into the Finger Lakes district of upstate New York to Canandaigua and on to Lake Ontario.

Yet there was more to the river than its commercial attractions. Perhaps because of its very name, the Susquehanna held a romantic, almost mystical appeal for overseas writers and artists. Just nine years before Emma's birth, some of England's greatest romantic poets were eyeing the Susquehanna Valley as a new

Zion, a place for the realization of a utopian ideal in an untamed, unspoiled wilderness of exciting new hopes and dreams—a new life in a new world! Such was the germ that flowered in Robert Southey and Samuel Taylor Coleridge's mutually conceived idealistic plan of "socialistic regeneration," which they called *Pantisocracy*, a word they invented, meaning "equality." While Southey perceived this utopia on the basis of a radical new secular economy, Coleridge, in rejecting Southey's atheism, justified the scheme on biblical grounds. Just as the early Christians had "all things common" and "sold their possessions and goods, and parted them to all men, as every man had need" (Acts 2:44–45), so too would they. Accumulating wealth would not be their goal; instead, they would work for the betterment of one another, to live and write together in love and a new harmony.

Enlisting the help and commitment of such other poets as Thomas Poole, Robert Lovell, and George Burnet, their plan called for a dozen men and their wives to charter a ship in 1795 and sail to America, where they would establish an agricultural and literary society somewhere in the wilderness of Pennsylvania. In his poem "Monody on Chatterton," a tribute to the young poet Thomas Chatterton, who had recently died, Coleridge mused:

> *Yet I will love to follow the sweet dream,*
> *Where Susquehanna pours his untamed stream,*
> *And on some hill, whose forest-frowning side*
> *Waves o'er the murmurs of his calmer tide;*
> *And I will build a cenotaph to thee,*
> *Sweet harper of time-shrouded minstrelsy.*[1]

Why they aimed for the Susquehanna River Valley is not clear. Joseph Cottle, Coleridge's Bristol publisher and lifelong supporter, remembered, "It seemed to rise solely from its imposing name, which, if not classical was at least poetical."[2] But Thomas Cooper, Joseph Priestley's son-in-law, had been to America and suggested the valley, where he had hopes of selling land at bargain prices. Sufficient funds for Pantisocracy never materialized, however, and with opposition mounting from in-laws and friends, the plan was indefinitely postponed. Their Susquehanna Zion would have to wait. Before Coleridge passed away in 1834, another "sweet dream" at the Susquehanna was coming to pass.

"We Still Continued the Work of Translation"

The circumstances during which Joseph Smith and Oliver Cowdery translated the Book of Mormon were most trying and difficult. With funds given them from Martin Harris, Joseph and Emma had moved from Palmyra to Harmony, Pennsylvania, into the small house Emma's brother Jesse had built near her parents and had vacated when he moved west to Illinois. The young couple negotiated to buy the house and thirteen acres of land over time for two hundred dollars. Meanwhile, feelings remained strained between Joseph and his father-in-law, who never quite forgave him for eloping with his daughter in January 1827. When Emma and Joseph Smith met up with Isaac after their elopement, "The old man tearfully rebuked Joseph for stealing his daughter and said he would rather follow her to her grave than have her married to Joseph."[3] Nor could Isaac shake his conviction that Joseph was a drifter, a ne'er-do-well gold digger from his silver mining days working for Josiah Stowell of nearby South Bainbridge, New York.

Emma had underestimated the opposition she and her husband would receive from her family. "[Joseph's] wife's father and family were all against him and would not help him," biographers of Emma Smith have noted. On more than one occasion, Joseph and Emma had to travel the twenty-eight miles upriver to the home of Joseph Knight Sr. in Colesville, New York, to ask for assistance—"some little provisions"—and on one occasion a pair of shoes and three dollars.[4]

Emma's parents were not the only ones making life difficult for Joseph and Emma. At one point the intransigent and unpredictable Lucy Harris, wife of Martin Harris, ransacked "every nook and corner" of Emma's house looking for the gold plates or any other physical evidence of the authenticity of the Book of Mormon. The two women never got along with each other. And it was also here that on 15 June 1828, after an exhaustive labor, Emma tragically lost her firstborn child, Alvin, when he was only three hours old.[5]

And during much of the summer, Joseph labored under the chastisement of heaven until he was again ready to continue the work of translation. Thus when Oliver Cowdery arrived on the scene on 5 April 1829, he must have sensed that they would be working under the shadow of disapproval and distrust from the Hale family. They received precious few supplies or even encouragement from any of the Hale family or from nearby residents and Hale family friends.

Nonetheless, with a renewed sense of commission and boundless enthusiasm, the two men eagerly began their translation work 7 April 1829. Considering that they completed the entire Book of Mormon by 1 July, a maximum of eighty-five days, they translated at the astonishing speed of approximately six to seven published pages per day with little time for corrections. Having learned how to use the Urim and Thummim from his previous work with Martin Harris on the 116 pages of the book of Lehi and having been taught to live by heaven in order to bring forth the record of heaven, Joseph Smith was prepared to translate and dictate at a formidable pace.

It is not given from the historical record for us to know precisely what Book of Mormon passages prompted Joseph and Oliver to prayerfully inquire into the matter of baptism. Considering the careful tutoring Joseph had thus far received in gospel principles, he would not have been ignorant of this essential ordinance. The angel Moroni had been instructing him annually on "what the Lord was going to do" and "how and in what manner" he would conduct his kingdom in the last days (Joseph Smith–History 1:54). Joseph may also have been concerned with his own recurring desire for the remission of sins and how he, in a world without divine authority, could participate in such an ordinance. Thus he and Oliver Cowdery went forth in faith and earnest expectation, even anxious anticipation. They seemed to sense that the next chapter was about to unfold in the ongoing curriculum of Restoration schooling.

Of this anticipation, President Joseph F. Smith, the Prophet's nephew, wrote that while Joseph and Oliver were engaged in the work of translation, they became "animated over the truths and glorious promises unfolded to them in their work, and desired to reach out after these blessings." Yet the Lord "gently admonished them not to be in a hurry; he said: 'You must wait yet a little while, for ye are not yet ordained,' but the promise was given that they should be ordained thereafter, and they should go forth and deliver the word of God unto the children of men."[6]

How much of the Book of Mormon the two men had translated by mid-May 1829 is guesswork. If, as now seems likely, they began at or near the book of Mosiah,[7] after just one or two weeks of translating they would have already covered the four great sermonizers of that book: King Benjamin and his remarkable discourse on faith and service (Mosiah 2–6), Abinadi and his repeated calls for repentance (Mosiah 11–16), Alma and his teachings on baptism in the wilderness by the waters of Mormon (Mosiah 18); and finally Alma the Younger and the need for a spiritual rebirth (Mosiah 27). They had probably reached 3 Nephi with its account of the coming of Christ to the Nephites and his teachings on baptism: "Verily I say unto you, that whoso repenteth of his sins through your words, and desireth to be baptized in my name, on this wise shall ye baptize them—Behold, ye shall go down and stand in the water, and in my name shall ye baptize them. . . . And according as I have commanded you thus shall ye baptize. And there shall be no disputations among you, as there have hitherto been" (3 Nephi 11:23, 28). Whether it was this or some other scripture, Joseph does not say, but baptism and the authority to perform such was clearly a topic of concern. "We still continued the work of translation," he recorded, "when, in the ensuing month (May, 1829), we on a certain day went into the woods to pray and inquire of the Lord respecting baptism for the remission of sins, that we found mentioned in the translation of the plates" (Joseph Smith–History 1:68).

"Fruits Meet for Repentance"

The first principles and ordinances of the gospel of Jesus Christ are so interwoven and interconnected that, like the patchwork of a quilt or the colors of a rainbow, they cannot be understood in isolation from one another. They are a compound in one, a pattern of living—one principle leading to another.

In the early Christian church, baptism was taught as essential to the gospel plan. John the Baptist baptized Christ in the

River Jordan "to fulfil all righteousness" (Matthew 3:15). Christ, in turn, taught that "except a man be born of water and of the Spirit, he cannot enter into the kingdom of God" (John 3:5). Paul the apostle, after his glorious vision of Christ while on the road to Damascus, went to be healed, baptized, and taught by "a certain disciple . . . named Ananias" (Acts 9:10), the human instrument of God's miracle.

The ordinance of baptism, therefore, emanates from faith in Christ and repentance and is the gateway to receiving the gift of the Holy Ghost. "And he commandeth all men that they must repent, and be baptized in his name, having perfect faith in the Holy One of Israel" (2 Nephi 9:23). A command of God, baptism is the fulfillment of humility and contrition, the blossom of repentance, and the signification or sealing of one's desire to "return unto [Christ] with full purpose of heart" (3 Nephi 10:6). Mormon elaborated on this natural sequence of principles when he wrote, "And the first fruits of repentance is baptism; and baptism cometh by faith unto the fulfilling the commandments; and the fulfilling the commandments bringeth remission of sins; and the remission of sins bringeth meekness, and . . . the visitation of the Holy Ghost" (Moroni 8:25–26). Baptism means to strive to put away sin, to covenant to take upon oneself the name of Christ, and to become a new creature in him.

And if "faith unto repentance" (Alma 34:15) leads to baptism and receiving the gift of the Holy Ghost, baptism leads to continual repentance—a continuing, upward cycle of remission of sins and an onward progression to eternal life. "I indeed baptize you with water unto repentance," John the Baptist declared and instructed his followers to "bring forth therefore fruits meet for repentance" (Matthew 3:8, 11). Wrote Alma: "Ye must repent, and be born again; for the Spirit saith if ye are not born again ye cannot inherit the kingdom of heaven; therefore come and be baptized unto repentance, that ye may be washed from your sins, that ye may have faith on the Lamb of God, who taketh away the sins of the world, who is mighty to save and to cleanse from all unrighteousness" (Alma 7:14). Thus baptism opens the way to a life of continual repentance, the mercy of forgiveness, and the abiding presence of the Holy Ghost, which in turn lead to an everlasting increase of joy and happiness.

The weekly partaking of the sacrament is an opportunity to renew the covenant of baptism and, in return, to have the blessings of baptism—the remission of sin—restored on a weekly basis. The sacrament is taken weekly in remembrance of the flesh and blood of Christ as a token and covenant that we will "always remember him and keep his commandments which he has given [us]; that [we] may always have his Spirit to be with [us]" (D&C 20:77; Moroni 4:3). Said Elder Dallin H. Oaks: "The sacrament of the Lord's Supper is a renewal of the covenants and blessings of baptism. . . . When we comply with this covenant, the Lord renews the cleansing effect of our baptism. We are made clean and can always have His Spirit to be with us."[8] Thus through the sacrament, the effect of the covenant and ordinance of baptism is renewed over and over again. Though a simple and unadorned ordinance, the sacrament constitutes the center of weekly Latter-day Saint worship, the constant renewal of the baptismal covenant and a recurring remission of sin through the continuing grace of Christ.

The blessing of baptism and its remission of sins is made possible only through the atonement of Christ and the priesthood authority of those officiating. It is so sacred a blessing that it is a personal covenant, one witnessed by others, to live by every word of Christ. As with physical birth and the reception of one's parental surname, baptism marks a person's birth into the divine nature of Christ and the taking of his name. King Benjamin declared, "There shall be no other name given nor any other way nor means whereby salvation can come unto the children of men, only in and through the name of Christ, the Lord Omnipotent" (Mosiah 3:17). Through baptism, we become "Christ-ians" or, as C. S. Lewis reverently put it, "little Christs."[9] From there, we grow, in Paul's phraseology, "unto a perfect man, unto the measure of the stature of the fulness of Christ" (Ephesians 4:13).

Nephi summed up these principles when he wrote, "Wherefore, my beloved brethren, I know that if ye shall follow the Son, with full purpose of heart, acting no hypocrisy and no deception before God, but with real intent, repenting of your sins, witnessing unto the Father that ye are willing to take upon you the name of Christ, by baptism—yea, by following your Lord and your Savior down into the water, according to his word, behold, then shall ye receive the Holy Ghost" (2 Nephi 31:13).

"Upon You My Fellow Servants"

While Joseph Smith and Oliver Cowdery were "employed, praying and calling upon the Lord" (Joseph Smith–History 1:68) near Harmony, Pennsylvania, on or near the banks of the Susquehanna River on 15 May 1829, what B. H. Roberts once called the "Third Vision" opened to their view.[10] Yet another messenger appeared, this time John the Baptist, who, after descending in a cloud of light, laid his hands upon them and ordained them, saying: "Upon you my fellow servants, in the name of Messiah, I confer the Priesthood of Aaron, which holds the keys of the ministering of angels, and of the gospel of repentance, and of baptism by immersion for the remission of sins; and this shall never be taken again from the earth until the sons of Levi do offer again an offering unto the Lord in righteousness" (Joseph Smith–History 1:69; D&C 13). Oliver Cowdery, who was the first to tell the account of John's appearance, wrote, "On a sudden, as from the midst of eternity, the voice of the Redeemer spake peace to us, while the vail was parted and the angel of God came down clothed with glory, and delivered the anxiously looked for message, and the keys of the gospel of repentance."[11]

Conferring upon them both the keys of the Aaronic Priesthood—that is, the keys to repentance and of the ministering of angels and also the power and authority to baptize—this angel from on high, acting "under the direction of Peter, James and John," commanded them "to go and be baptized" (Joseph Smith–History 1:72, 70). In his dual role of priesthood restorer as well as a tutor in the principles of the gospel, John the Baptist taught them the true order of baptism. He gave them specific "directions that I [Joseph] should baptize Oliver Cowdery, and that afterwards he should baptize me" (Joseph Smith–History 1:70), which the two men promptly did. The fact that the angel himself did not baptize signifies that an earthly or physical ordinance must be performed by those in their mortal state.

The restoration of priesthood authority, as President Joseph F. Smith once remarked, was an indispensable prerequisite to the validity of their imminent baptism. "No ordinance of the gospel can be performed acceptably to God or with efficacy to man except by its authority and power, and certainly there is no ordinance or rite instituted by the Almighty in the great plan of redemption which is not essential to the salvation or exaltation of his children."[12] Whether this heavenly messenger stayed to witness and validate the actual performance of the ordinance is not clear,[13] but the implication is that as their teacher and instructor, he did.[14]

Oliver could not refrain from painting the following picture of what occurred and the attendant emotions they felt at the time: "'Twas the voice of an angel from glory, 'twas a message from the Most High! And as we heard we rejoiced, while His love enkindled upon our souls, and we were wrapped in the vision of the Almighty! . . . What joy filled our hearts.

" . . . I shall not attempt to paint to you the feelings of this heart, nor the majestic beauty and glory which surrounded us on this occasion; but . . . earth, nor men . . . cannot begin to clothe language in as interesting and sublime a manner as this holy personage . . . and I shall ever look upon this expression of the Savior's goodness with wonder and thanksgiving" (Joseph Smith–History, 1:71, note).

Just as Moroni was ideally suited to teach his apprentice prophet all things pertaining to the Book of Mormon and the principle of repentance, could there have been a more suitable instructor in the ordinance of baptism for the remission of sins than John the Baptist? He was the singular individual who, while in mortality, had baptized the Son of God and held the keys of the Aaronic Priesthood in the former dispensation. Surely it is the quality of the teachers of the Restoration, as well as their prophesied coming, that is so impressive about the divine faculty and curriculum of the Restoration.

Of the suitability of these angelic tutors and the applicability of their message, Elder B. H. Roberts wrote: "When the work reached that stage of development that men could be taught repentance, and receive baptism for the remission of sins, who so qualified or who with more propriety could be sent to deliver the keys of the priesthood that is especially appointed to cry repentance and administer baptism than *the* teacher of repentance and *the* Baptist? . . . It was of course working to a well-matured plan, but the plan existed in the mind of God; and it was given to Joseph Smith piece-meal—incident following incident without an apparent suspicion in his mind that each incident was a step in the progress of the mighty march of events matured in the mind of God. . . . The consistency and appropriateness of the development Joseph Smith never spoke of; it was left for others to note these things after the work was well advanced in the course of its development."[15]

And further, on the peculiar relevancy of the appearance of John the Baptist, Elder James E. Talmage commented: "The question of this man's [Joseph's] divine commission is a challenging one to the world today. If his claims to a divine appointment be false, forming as they do the foundation of the Church in this the last dispensation, the superstructure cannot be stable; if, however, his avowed ordination under the hands of heavenly personages be a fact, one need search no farther for the cause of the phenomenal vitality and continuous development of the restored Church."[16]

"There Hath Not Risen a Greater Than John the Baptist"

Cousin to the Savior, John was born to parents who had themselves been taught divine principles of faith and repentance. Reprimanded by the angel Gabriel for disbelieving that his wife, Elisabeth, Mary's faithful cousin, would bear a son, Zacharias had been struck dumb until Elisabeth, who was well past her childbearing years, bore the son whom Zacharias called John, as commanded by the angel. By the power of the Holy Ghost, Zacharias then prophesied of John's special mission: "To give knowledge of salvation unto his people by the remission of their sins" (Luke 1:77)—or in other words, to teach the gospel of baptism. Thus John had been taught by devout and believing parents who, having themselves been taught of heaven, raised him in the confidence of the Lord.

As to his unique mission, both ancient and modern scripture provide abundant insight. The special calling of John the Baptist did not end with his execution at the hands of the wicked King Herod and Herodias, his step-niece and partner in adultery. Declared Zacharias at the time of his son's birth: "And thou, child, shalt be called the prophet of the Highest; for thou shalt go before the face of the Lord to prepare his ways; to give knowledge of salvation unto his people by the remission of their sins, through the tender mercy of our God; whereby the dayspring from on high hath visited us, to give light to them that sit in darkness and in the shadow of death, to guide our feet into the way of peace. And the child grew, and waxed strong in spirit, and was in the deserts till the day of his shewing unto Israel" (Luke 1:76–80).

Upon his coming forth out of the wilderness in the due time of the Lord, John baptized thousands of believing Jews. As forerunner of the Christ, he was the rightful high priest of the Levitical Priesthood and held the keys of the Aaronic Priesthood.

"It was John the Baptist who held the *presidency* of this priesthood in the days of his ministry as the forerunner of Jesus Christ," wrote Joseph Fielding Smith. "As a Levite, with his authority coming to him by divine right of descent, John was the rightful *presiding priest of the Aaronic order in Israel.* This authority had come to him by lineage, and the Lord has made it known that John 'was baptized while he was yet in his childhood, and was ordained by the angel of God at the time he was eight days old . . .' (D&C 84:28).

"Had the Church of God been in existence with the Jews in that day, instead of the Jews being in a dreadful state of apostasy, then John the Baptist would have taken his proper place as the presiding priest of the Aaronic order. But they recognized him not and failed to understand his authority, even as they failed to comprehend the authority of our Lord. The authority of John was that which was conferred upon Aaron and which came down by right of lineage to Eleazar and his posterity after him; but the Jews failed to recognize John and rejected him. By right of his authority John laid the foundation for the overthrow of their kingdom, or power, which was based on a false foundation. Had they accepted John then also would they have accepted Christ, the Lord, their rightful King and the great High Priest of their salvation."[17]

"I indeed baptize you with water unto repentance," John said to his disciples, "but he that cometh after me is mightier than I, whose shoes I am not worthy to bear: he shall baptize you with the Holy Ghost, and with fire" (Matthew 3:11). Joseph Smith, in commenting in January 1843 on John the Baptist, said, "No man could have better authority to administer than John; and our Savior submitted to that authority Himself, by being baptized by John; therefore the Kingdom of God was set up on the earth, even in the days of John."[18]

The supreme moment in John's ministry occurred when Jesus came from Galilee to Jordan to be baptized of John. "But John forbad him, saying, I have need to be baptized of thee, and comest thou to me? And Jesus answering said unto him, Suffer it to be so now: for thus it becometh us to fulfil all righteousness. Then he suffered him. And Jesus, when he was baptized, went up straightway out of the water: and lo, the heavens were opened unto him, and he saw the Spirit of God descending like a dove, and lighting upon him: And lo a voice from heaven, saying, This is my beloved Son, in whom I am well pleased" (Matthew 3:13–17).

In further discoursing on the Baptist, Joseph remarked that John's greatness consisted of being "entrusted with a divine mission of preparing the way before the face of the Lord" and "to baptize the Son of Man." Joseph then asked, "Whoever had so great a privilege and glory?" Only John the Baptist, Joseph answered, who "was the only legal administrator in the affairs of the kingdom there was then on the earth."[19] A man of meekness, humility, and courage, John at first demurred from baptizing Jesus because he fully recognized who He was: not merely a relative or a great teacher but God himself—the God of Abraham, Isaac, and Jacob; Jehovah, the God of the Old Testament; the very Creator of the world; the Word made flesh. When Jesus heard of the beheading of John through the treachery of King Herod and Herodias, he immediately left his apostles and the thronging multitudes "by ship into a desert place apart" (Matthew 14:13). Christ's tribute to John, who had sacrificed his life in declaring repentance, is well-known in scripture: "Among them that are born of women there hath not risen a greater than John the Baptist: notwithstanding he that is least in the kingdom of heaven is greater than he" (Matthew 11:11).

Modern scripture elaborates on John's three-fold mission: "For he was baptized while he was yet in his childhood, and was ordained by the angel of God at the time he was eight days old unto this power, to overthrow the kingdom of the Jews, and to make straight the way of the Lord before the face of his people, to prepare them for the coming of the Lord, in whose hand is given all power" (D&C 84:28). The first two commissions were fulfilled during his mortal ministry; the third one was perhaps completed with his visit to the Susquehanna in preparation for the Second Coming.

At the Mount of Transfiguration, where Christ was prepared in all things pertaining to his pending "decease which he should accomplish at Jerusalem" (Luke 9:31), Moses and Elias appeared unto him. Whether that Elias was John the Baptist is not told in scripture,[20] but Christ certainly used the occasion to prophesy of John's later mission when he would return to prepare the people of the last days for the coming of the Lord. "And Jesus answered and said unto them, Elias truly shall first come, and restore all things. But I say unto you, That Elias is come already, and they knew him not, but have done unto him whatsoever they listed. Likewise shall also the Son of man suffer of them. Then the disciples understood that he spake unto them of John the Baptist" (Matthew 17:11–13).

Thus the "Third Vision" of the Restoration, in which was taught the third principle and first ordinance of the gospel, came as fulfillment of prophecy, though it did not come until Joseph and Oliver had been well schooled in faith and repentance, both of which are prerequisites to baptism. Unspoken, yet so obviously taught in this vision, was the doctrine of the resurrection. For John the Baptist was here a glorified, resurrected personage. "Can you imagine what a wonderful experience it must have been for Joseph Smith and Oliver Cowdery when John the Baptist spoke to them?" asked President Gordon B. Hinckley. "Here was a man who had lived upon the earth more than 1800 years earlier. Now he was speaking to two young men while he held his hands upon their heads. His was a resurrected body. Theirs were mortal bodies. They felt his hands, the materiality of them, and understood the words which he spoke. This tells us that resurrected beings are tangible, that they can move and act, that they can speak and be understood."[21] Clearly the restoration of the Aaronic Priesthood was also reaffirmation both of Christ's resurrection from the tomb and of the subsequent resurrection of others.

"The Holy Ghost Fell upon Him"

After they had been baptized, they ordained one another to the Aaronic Priesthood, Joseph ordaining Oliver first and then Oliver ordaining Joseph—"for so we were commanded." The two men, now endowed with a remission of their sins, were in a position to receive "great and glorious blessings from our Heavenly Father" and to be taught by the master teacher and revelator, the Holy Ghost, who was about to take over where angels had left off. For no sooner had Joseph Smith baptized Oliver "than the Holy Ghost fell upon him, and he stood up and prophesied many things which should shortly come to pass" (Joseph Smith–History 1:71, 73). If Oliver Cowdery prophesied by the Holy Ghost of things shortly to come, Joseph Smith, after he had been baptized, "also had the spirit of prophecy" and "prophesied concerning the rise of this Church, and many other things connected with the Church, and this generation of the children of men." Again, the experience was a highly emotive one, the two being "filled with the Holy Ghost, and rejoiced in the God of our salvation" (Joseph Smith–History 1:73).

The gift of the Holy Ghost would not be conferred upon them until the restoration of the Melchizedek Priesthood some time later, but the moment of their baptism pointed to the indispensable role that the Holy Ghost would play in the teaching and training of these first students of the Restoration. "Our minds being now enlightened, we began to have the scriptures laid open to our understandings, and the true meaning and intention of their more mysterious passages revealed unto us in a manner which we never could attain to previously, nor ever before had thought of" (Joseph Smith–History 1:74).

For the previous several months, Joseph had been using the

Urim and Thummim, or "interpreters" (Mosiah 8:13), which had been indispensable in translating the Book of Mormon. They had also acted as a guide and conduit for receiving revelations (see D&C 3, 6–7, 11). And yet it was the power of the Holy Ghost that was now revealing the true meaning of the scriptures to their understanding. Such a process would serve as a template for prophetic revelation to modern prophets and apostles to interpret and apply sacred writ to the modern Church. For it has ever been the Holy Ghost who bears witness, who reveals all things, who testifies of Christ and "bring[s] all things to [our] remembrance" (John 14:26). Far more than a return of angelic visitors, as great as they were in their prophesied times and seasons, the Restoration was a revelation of the Godhead—God the Father, God the Son, and now, in greater measure, God the Holy Ghost. Just as the Holy Ghost had manifested himself in the sign of a dove at the River Jordan at the Savior's baptism, so he once again manifested himself at the Susquehanna, attesting to God's modern miracle in this "uttermost part of the earth" (Acts 1:8)

Soon after this glorious moment in Church history, Joseph Smith and Oliver Cowdery baptized a few others, including Samuel H. Smith, Joseph's younger brother, on 25 May 1829. Samuel had come to Harmony earlier with Oliver to help Joseph till his land and put in a spring crop. Hyrum Smith, who came from Palmyra afterward "to know what the Lord would have him do," was the recipient of a revelation of guidance and comfort (D&C 11). He also was baptized, not in the Susquehanna but in Seneca Lake, Fayette Township, New York, in June by his younger brother Joseph. Later, once the Church had been organized, Samuel and Hyrum were rebaptized not only for the remission of sins but also preparatory to their confirmation as members of the newly formed Church. While one may assume that Joseph and

Oliver were likewise rebaptized, no confirmation of that event has yet been found.[22]

"There Will Be Great Rejoicing"

It is not without consequence that Oliver Cowdery, "the second elder" of the Church (D&C 20:3), fell away and was excommunicated from the Church during the dark and troubling days of Kirtland, Ohio, and Far West, Missouri, in 1838. The details of his disaffection and excommunication are perhaps not as important to this study as are his return and rebaptism. Thanks to the intrepid efforts of Phineas Young, brother to Brigham Young, Oliver was kept conversant with the affairs of the Saints. As a lawyer first in Ohio and then in Wisconsin, Oliver even offered his services to the Prophet Joseph Smith when he was incarcerated in Carthage Jail in June 1844. Plagued with tuberculosis and sensing that his health was declining, Oliver returned to the Saints at Kanesville, Iowa, in November 1848. When Brigham Young, then in the valley of the Great Salt Lake, heard of his return, he penned these memorable lines of sincere gratitude and earnest invitation:

"We impose [on] the present moment . . . to express to you our unbounded confidence and joy in those principles and doctrines of the Church of Jesus Christ of Latter Day Saints, which we have so long taught and practiced, amid scenes of persecution and blood, and many of which, in former days, we have listened to with delight from your lips, and to the truth of which, we have heard you testify with unshaken confidence. . . . And say to you in the spirit of Jesus, and by the calling whereunto we have been called, Come, for all things are now ready, and the Spirit and the Bride say Come: and return to our Father's house, from whence thou hast wandered, and partake of the fatted calf, and sup and be filled: and again be ordained with the jewels of salvation, and be shod with the preparation of the Gospel of Peace . . . and renew thy testimony to the Truth of the Book of Mormon with a loud voice and faithful heart and you will soon feel the Holy Ghost burning in your bones like fire in the dry stubble, thy soul will be filled with rejoicing, and you will again cry aloud, verily it is good to serve the Lord for his mercy endureth forever: and there will be great rejoicing in thy Father's house, for he will embrace thee with the kisses of many blessings.

"And the Saints [his sons and daughters] will with open arms hail thee as their long lost brother found in the new and everlasting covenant."[23]

At the monthly meeting of the high priests in the Kanesville Log Tabernacle on 5 November 1848, Oliver Cowdery was given liberty by Orson Hyde, presiding officer in the region, to address the hushed gathering. Oliver bore his testimony of the Book of Mormon, "that the Priesthood was with this people; and the Twelve were the only men that could lead the Church, after the death of Joseph. [He] seemed to possess an excellent spirit." A few days later, he again called upon the Saints and sought rebaptism. "I have not come to seek place, nor to interfere with the business and calling of those men who have borne the burthen since the death of Joseph. I throw myself at your feet, and wish to be one of your number and be a mere member of the Church and my mere asking to be rebaptized is an end to all pretensions to authority."[24]

"I feel that I can honorably return," he said. "I have sustained an honorable character before the world during my absence from you, this though a small matter with you, it is of vast importance. I have ever had the honor of the Kingdom in view, and men are to be judged by the testimony given. I feel to sanction what has been said here today. I am out of the church. I know the door into the church, and I wish to become a member through the door. I wish to be a humble private member. I did not come here to seek honor."[25]

Oliver also said: "Bro. Hyde has just said that it was all important that we keep in the true channel in order to avoid the sandbars. This is true. The channel is here. The priesthood is here."[26]

After a unanimous vote of the quorum of high priests and all present, permission was granted that he be readmitted to the Church. One week later, on 12 November 1848, almost twenty years since the coming of John the Baptist, Oliver Cowdery was rebaptized by Orson Hyde. Thus even in his coming back to the Church after a decade of estrangement, the Church's second elder once again taught the importance of humbling oneself and of receiving the ordinance of baptism.

Conclusion

Today The Church of Jesus Christ of Latter-day Saints has erected a monument near the banks of the Susquehanna River in commemoration of the restoration of the Aaronic Priesthood and its attendant keys of authority by the resurrected John the Baptist. It marks the place where heaven touched earth, where the resurrection connected once again with mortality, and where the River Jordan and the Susquehanna share so much in common. It is a place where prophecy and history converged in a restoration of essential truths and saving ordinances.

In this "Third Vision" of the Restoration, Joseph Smith and Oliver Cowdery were taught of heaven in the first principles and ordinances of the gospel of Jesus Christ. The repeated efficacy of baptism and the renewal of forgiveness and remission of sins for Latter-day Saints come as they always have—through earnest faith, sincere repentance, baptism, and the weekly, worthily partaking of the sacrament. Far more than a mere one-time performance, baptism is a way of life, a never-ending keeping of covenants, a harbinger of better things to come. Indispensable to the Restoration, as so well taught by the divine messenger, John the Baptist, who in his mortal life baptized the Savior of the world, baptism remains the gateway to the ever-brighter promises of lasting joy and eternal happiness.

Chapter Four

HAVE YE RECEIVED THE HOLY GHOST?

The Comforter, which is the Holy Ghost,
whom the Father will send in my name, he shall teach
you all things, and bring all things to your remembrance,
whatsoever I have said unto you.

JOHN 14:26

The baptism of Joseph Smith and Oliver Cowdery was a necessary precursor to the decisive role the Holy Ghost would now begin to play in the Restoration. "No sooner had I baptized Oliver Cowdery, than the Holy Ghost fell upon him," Joseph recorded, "and he stood up and prophesied many things which should shortly come to pass." And as soon as Joseph was baptized under Oliver's hands, he also "had the spirit of prophecy" and "prophesied concerning the rise of this Church, and many other things connected with the Church, and this generation of the children of men." Both men were "filled with the Holy Ghost, and rejoiced in the God of our salvation" (Joseph Smith–History 1:73).

By this same spirit manifested to them on 15 May 1829, they began to have the scriptures laid open to their understanding, and "the true meaning and intention of their more mysterious passages revealed unto [them] in a manner which [they] never could attain to previously, nor ever before had thought of" (Joseph Smith–History 1:74). Building on Moroni's teachings and careful explanations of scripture and also the Prophet's experience in using the Urim and Thummim in translating the Book of Mormon, the Holy Ghost, in his capacity as witness and revelator, now began to assume in ever greater proportion his role as the master teacher of the Prophet of the Restoration. The revelation of John the Baptist and the restoration of the Aaronic Priesthood on 15 May 1829 was a preparation for the gift of the Holy Ghost, which could only come after the restoration of Melchizedek Priesthood authority under the hands of Peter, James, and John.

"The Voice of Peter, James, and John"

The exact date and place of the restoration of this higher priesthood authority, what Elder B. H. Roberts called the "Fourth Vision" of the Restoration, have yet to be discovered; however, there are definite clues.[1] That it did not come in Fayette or Palmyra is clear from the following revelation: "The voice of Peter, James, and John in the wilderness between Harmony, Susquehanna county, and Colesville, Broome county, on the Susquehanna river, declaring themselves as possessing the keys of the kingdom, and of the dispensation of the fulness of times" (D&C 128:20). Just where the precise spot was between Harmony and Colesville, a distance of twenty-seven miles, is impossible to say.

In an 1882 letter to President Joseph F. Smith, Addison Everett, a bishop of the Church in Winter Quarters and again later in Salt Lake City, recalled hearing the Prophet in Nauvoo relate the circumstances surrounding the restoration of the Melchizedek Priesthood:

"Said as they were translating the Book of Mormon at his

father-in-law's in Susquehanna County Pennsylvania. They were threatened by a mob and in the same time Father Knight came down from Colesville County, New York, and desired them to go home with him and preach to them in his neighborhood and on account of the mob spirit prevailing they concluded to go." Everett recalled that even in Colesville persecution continued, forcing Joseph and Oliver to return to Harmony.

His letter continues: "And they wandered in a dense forest all night and oftentimes in mud and water up to their knees. And Brother Oliver got quite exhausted in the after part of the night and Brother Joseph had to put his arm around him and almost carry him. And just as the day broke in the east Brother Oliver gave out entirely and he, Br Joseph, leaned him against an oak tree just outside a field fence, Br Oliver crying out, 'How long, O Lord, O how long, Br Joseph, have we got to suffer these things?' Just this moment Peter, James & John came to us and ordained [us to] the Holy Apostleship and gave [unto] us the keys of the dispensation of the fullness of times. And we had some 16 or 17 miles to go to reach our place of residence and Brother Oliver could travel as well as I could. . . . Now as to time and place. I heard the name of the banks of the Susquehanna River spoken [of] but where it was placed I cannot tell. No doubt the oak tree and the field fence were adjacent to the river. As to time I cannot be very explicit. But as the mob spirit had not abated when they returned, they had to remove to Father Whitmer's [Fayette, Seneca County] to finish the translation."[2]

How much credence can be given to a reminiscence written almost forty years after the fact is debatable. Nonetheless, it is true that the Knights assisted in the translation with paper and provisions, that persecution attended the translation, that by 1 June 1829 Joseph and Oliver had removed north to Harmony, and that the two were never together again in the wilderness of the Susquehanna.

As for the matter of timing, as early as June 1829 the revelations speak of Joseph and Oliver having already received the apostleship. "And I speak unto you, even as unto Paul mine apostle, for you are called even with that same calling with which he was called" (D&C 18:9). The Articles and Covenants of the Church—section 20 of the Doctrine and Covenants—refer to Joseph and Oliver each as having already been "called of God, and ordained an apostle of Jesus Christ" (v. 2) some time before the Church was organized on 6 April 1830.[3] According to revelation given the day the Church was organized, Joseph had been "*inspired of the Holy Ghost* to lay the foundation thereof, and to build it up unto the most holy faith" (D&C 21:2; emphasis added). And again as per the Articles and Covenants of the Church, no officer in the Church—whether elder, priest, teacher, or deacon—could be ordained unless "by the power of the Holy Ghost, which *is in the one* who ordains him" (D&C 20:60; emphasis added). Put another way, there could have been no ordinations and no Church without first the bestowal of the gift of the Holy Ghost upon the first and second elders of the Church. As President George Q. Cannon remarked: "[Joseph] was unable to seal the gift of the Holy Ghost, or to ordain an elder, until after Peter, James and John had endowed him with the priesthood after the holy order of Melchizedek."[4]

Unlike their record of their baptism under the direction of John the Baptist, Joseph and Oliver recorded little about the formal bestowal of the Holy Ghost upon them, although Oliver years later was said to have confirmed its occurrence. "I was present with Joseph when an holy angel from God came down from heaven and conferred or restored the Aaronic Priesthood. . . . I was also present with Joseph when the Melchizedek priesthood was conferred by the holy angels of God—this was the more necessary."[5] President J. Reuben Clark Jr. suggested that "Peter, James and John appeared to Joseph Smith and Oliver Cowdery and conferred upon them, ordained them to, the higher, or Melchizedek Priesthood, by a ceremony equivalent to that by which the Aaronic Priesthood was restored."[6] Thus, Peter, James, and John acted in accordance with the previous pattern in conferring the Melchizedek Priesthood upon both men. Now endowed with the necessary authority, the two men bestowed upon each other the gift of the Holy Ghost, though formal confirmation would have to wait until the Church was organized.

Surely one of the critical purposes of the restoration of the Melchizedek Priesthood was to authorize the ordinance of the laying on of hands for the gift of the Holy Ghost. Elder Orson Pratt explained: "The Lord sent messengers from heaven with a higher priesthood . . . , whose names were Peter, James and John, three ancient Apostles, and they conferred upon them [Joseph Smith and Oliver Cowdery] the priesthood and Apostleship that they themselves had, which gave them authority not only to baptize, but to administer in the ordinance of the Holy Ghost by the laying on of hands in the name of Jesus, precisely the same as the Apostles did when on the earth."[7]

The gift of the Holy Ghost was to be given only to those Saints who were "added to the church" as in New Testament times (Acts 2:47). It was to be the resident power of the believer, the promised gift of the Messiah to those who take up his cross and accept membership in his Church and cause. Thus the reestablishment and organization of his true Church was made possible only through the restoration of priesthood authority.

"All Things to Your Remembrance"

In similar fashion to that of the New Testament apostles, Joseph Smith may not have fully understood the deep significance of the experiences he had witnessed between 1820 and 1829 until he too had received the gift of the Holy Ghost, who is the great teacher, tutor, and divine mentor in all things pertaining to the gospel of Jesus Christ. And if true with Joseph Smith, it was certainly so with his faithful followers: "Ye are not able to abide the presence of God now, neither the ministering of angels; wherefore, continue in patience until ye are perfected. Let not your minds turn back; and when ye are worthy, in mine own due time, ye shall see and know that which was conferred upon you by the hands of my servant Joseph Smith, Jun." (D&C 67:13–14).

Before Christ ended his mortal ministry, he promised his apostles that he would not leave them comfortless, but that after his departure he would send unto them "another Comforter" (John 14:16), or "the Spirit of Truth" (John 16:13). This "unspeakable gift of the Holy Ghost" (D&C 121:26), this divine endowment, would bring the apostles peace, hope, and the lasting power to endure all things and would teach them the full meaning of those principles that Christ had taught unto them. "It is expedient for you that I go away: for if I go not away, the Comforter will not come unto you; but if I depart, I will send him unto you" (John 16:7). When he came, he would bring all things to their remembrance that pertained to an understanding of gospel principles. "Howbeit when he, the Spirit of truth, is come, he will guide you into all truth" (John 16:13).

The arresting irony in the culmination of the teaching and conversion of the early Christian apostles is that even they, who had been with Christ almost daily for three years, may not have fully comprehended his divinity and their role in the divine drama of his life and death until after his ascension into heaven. Their conversion was incomplete without the reception of the gift of the Holy Ghost, which came upon them afterward. By this power they reflected upon and more thoroughly understood their days with Christ, wrote their inspired letters and scriptural accounts of what they had both seen and heard, endured the shame and persecution of the world, and gave valiant witness and powerful testimony of what they had experienced.

Speaking of the endowment of the Holy Ghost upon the apostles of Jerusalem, President Joseph F. Smith taught: "Just before the risen Redeemer left the earth he commanded his disciples to tarry in the city of Jerusalem until they should be endowed with power from on high. They did so, and agreeable to promise, the Comforter came whilst they were met together, filling their hearts with unspeakable joy, insomuch that they spake in tongues and prophesied; and the inspiring influence of this holy being accompanied them in all their ministerial duties, enabling them to perform the great mission to which they had been called by the Savior."[8]

Elder Matthew Cowley said: "It was after he left them that he sent the Holy Ghost to the Apostles. He didn't want those men to go on doing anything without help from heaven. Even though he had been with them those three years, when he left, he didn't want to leave them alone. You know they are human beings. They would start preaching error, doing something wrong. So he said, 'You wait at Jerusalem, and I will send you the comforter, the Holy Ghost.' So they waited at Jerusalem after Christ had gone back into heaven. Then he sent the Holy Ghost. Then they had help from heaven."[9]

Elder Orson Pratt referred to "the universality of the Holy

Spirit" as the "great main-spring or secret by which a personal Being can exercise Almighty power where He is not personally present."[10] And the Prophet Joseph Smith revealed: "The Father has a body of flesh and bones as tangible as man's; the Son also; but the Holy Ghost has not a body of flesh and bones, but is a personage of Spirit. Were it not so, the Holy Ghost could not dwell in us. A man may receive the Holy Ghost, and it may descend upon him and not tarry with him" (D&C 130:22–23).

"No Man Can Say That Jesus Is the Lord, but by the Holy Ghost"

Whereas faith, repentance, and baptism are principles leading one to the presence of God, the Holy Ghost, sometimes referred to as the third member of the Godhead, is the in-dwelling of divinity promised to those who love God, keep his commandments, and promise to serve him.[11] "The Holy Spirit of promise" (D&C 76:53; 88:3; Ephesians 1:13), as he is also called, is the promised result of our faith and obedience, the companionship needed to endure the world, and the surety of our ultimate salvation and exaltation.

The critical question asked by the New Testament apostles was not "Are you saved?" but rather, as Paul asked those who had been baptized only "unto John's baptism":

"Have ye received the Holy Ghost since ye believed? And they said unto him, We have not so much as heard whether there be any Holy Ghost.

"And he said unto them, Unto what then were ye baptized? And they said, Unto John's baptism.

"Then said Paul, John verily baptized with the baptism of repentance, saying unto the people, that they should believe on him which should come after him, that is, on Christ Jesus.

"When they heard this, they were baptized in the name of the Lord Jesus.

"And when Paul had laid his hands upon them, the Holy Ghost came on them; and they spake with tongues, and prophesied" (Acts 19:2–6).

The Prophet Joseph Smith, when speaking of the incompleteness of baptism without the reception of the Holy Ghost, explained it this way: "[One] might as well baptize a bag of sand as a man if not done in view of the getting of the Holy Ghost. Baptism by water is but half a baptism—and is good for nothing with[out] the other, the Holy Ghost."[12] On another occasion, when asked by Martin Van Buren, then president of the United States, how the Latter-day Saints differed from all other faiths, Joseph explained that "we differed in mode of baptism, and the gift of the Holy Ghost by the laying on of hands. All other considerations were contained in the gift of the Holy Ghost."[13]

Indeed the priesthood was restored in large measure so that this gift of the Holy Ghost could again be renewed and bestowed upon the souls of God's children today. Of this truth, the Prophet declared: "We believe in the gift of the Holy Ghost being enjoyed now, as much as it was in the Apostles' days; we believe that it is necessary to make and to organize the Priesthood, that no man can be called to fill any office in the ministry without it; we also believe in prophecy, in tongues, in visions, and in revelations, in gifts, and in healings; and that these things cannot be enjoyed without the gift of the Holy Ghost. . . . We believe in it in all its fullness and power, and greatness, and glory; but whilst we do this, we believe in it rationally, consistently, and scripturally, and not according to the wild vagaries, foolish notions and traditions of men."[14]

The writings and teachings of the apostles in Acts, Romans,

and 1 Corinthians are nothing less than a primer on the doctrine and necessity of the Holy Ghost and deserve our careful review. Peter clearly taught that there is no salvation in Christ without the precious gift of the Holy Ghost, which is the right and opportunity to have the Holy Ghost with us at all times and in all places so long as our thoughts, predispositions, and actions permit him to stay. Those hearing the apostles preach the gospel urgently asked, "Men and brethren, what shall we do?" Peter replied: "Repent, and be baptized every one of you in the name of Jesus Christ for the remission of sins, and ye shall receive the gift of the Holy Ghost. For the promise is unto you, and to your children, and to all that are afar off, even as many as the Lord our God shall call" (Acts 2:37–39).

The gift of the Holy Ghost, therefore, is the constant companionship of God, the "great grace" of Christ that "was upon them all" (Acts 4:33), the enabling spiritual power, and the divine wisdom and understanding wherein we come to know Christ and his resurrection and ultimately receive the promise of eternal life. Elder John A. Widtsoe said: "The gift of the Holy Ghost confers upon a person the right to receive, as he may desire and need, the presence, light, and intelligence of the Holy Ghost. It gives, as it were, an official claim upon the mighty assistance and comforting assurance of the Holy Ghost [but] . . . remains inoperative unless a person leads a worthy life."[15]

This gift is the seed and flower of personal testimony, and when one is filled with the Holy Ghost—for it comes by degrees through one's faithfulness and obedience—one may speak with boldness, joy, and authority of divine truths. "For what man knoweth the things of a man, save the spirit of man which is in him? even so the things of God knoweth no man, but the Spirit of God" (1 Corinthians 2:11). The Prophet Joseph added, "The gift of the Holy Ghost by the laying on of hands, cannot be received through the medium of any other principle than the principle of righteousness, for if the proposals are not complied with, it is of no use, but withdraws."[16]

Often referred to as "the Spirit of the Lord" (Acts 5:9) or "the Spirit of God" (Alma 7:5), the Holy Ghost is the avenue of revelation and knowledge of God, "the still small voice" (1 Nephi 17:45; D&C 85:6) of truth. When about to be slain for his faith, Stephen "being full of the Holy Ghost, looked up stedfastly into heaven, and saw the glory of God, and Jesus standing on the right hand of God" (Acts 7:55).

President Wilford Woodruff, a man of visions and revelations, explained the revelatory nature of the Holy Ghost this way: "The Holy Ghost . . . is different from the common Spirit of God [Light of Christ], which we are told lighteth every man that cometh into the world. The Holy Ghost is only given to men through their obedience to the Gospel of Christ; and every man who receives that Spirit has a comforter within—a leader to dictate and guide him. This Spirit reveals, day by day, to every man who has faith, those things which are for his benefit. As Job said, 'There is a spirit in man and the inspiration of the Almighty giveth it understanding.' It is this inspiration of God to His children in every age of the world that is one of the necessary gifts to sustain man and enable him to walk by faith, and to go forth and obey all the dictations and commandments and revelations which God gives to His children to guide and direct them in life."[17]

Ironically, as spiritual as this divine gift is, it comes only through the medium of an "oral blessing pronounced upon the candidate," accompanied by the laying on of hands—an intimate, physical ordinance by which the Spirit of the Lord is conferred upon and sealed within the soul of another.[18] Just as the physical acts of procreation and birth miraculously contribute to bringing forth life, so the very light of God is transmitted from one physical source to another. It is the spiritual birth spoken of by Christ: "Except a man be born of water and of the Spirit, he cannot enter into the kingdom of God" (John 3:5).

Yet it comes only by the laying on of hands, a physical ordinance. Of this we read: "That by reason of transgression cometh the fall, which fall bringeth death, and inasmuch as ye were born into the world by water, and blood, and the spirit, which I have made, and so became of dust a living soul, even so ye must be born again into the kingdom of heaven, of water, and of the Spirit, and be cleansed by blood, even the blood of mine Only Begotten; that ye might be sanctified from all sin, and enjoy the words of eternal life in this world, and eternal life in the world to come, even immortal glory; for by the water ye keep the commandment; by the Spirit ye are justified, and by the blood ye are sanctified" (Moses 6:59–60).

With such a spiritual rebirth by the medium of a material or physical agent, we receive the "record of heaven; the Comforter; the peaceable things of immortal glory; the truth of all things; that which quickeneth all things, which maketh alive all things; that which knoweth all things, and hath all power according to wisdom, mercy, truth, justice, and judgment" (Moses 6:61). This is the rebirth, the baptism of fire, Christ referred to when comparing the reception of the Holy Ghost to the birth of a child—through water, blood, and spirit.[19] That men and women may receive the influence and prompting of the Holy Ghost before receiving this ordinance is clear from the experience of Cornelius, the centurion, who went fasting to Peter at the instruction of an angel and by the Spirit before being baptized. Likewise those in Samaria who had believed on the teachings of Philip, had been baptized, and had been wrought upon by the Spirit of the Lord also sought the fulfilling of their faith under the hands of Peter and John. "Who, when they were come down, prayed for them, that they might receive the Holy Ghost: (For as yet he was fallen upon none of them: only they were baptized in the name of the Lord Jesus.) Then laid they their hands on them, and they received the Holy Ghost" (Acts 8:15–17).

Even Paul's remarkable conversion while on the road to Damascus and his vision of Christ were incomplete without his being baptized and receiving the Holy Ghost. Is it not instructive to note that Christ directed Paul—then named Saul—to "go into the street which is called Straight" (Acts 9:11) unto Ananias, an authorized representative of the Lord, to complete the intent of God's calling him? "And Ananias went his way, and entered into the house; and putting his hands on him said, Brother Saul, the Lord, even Jesus, that appeared unto thee in the way as thou camest, hath sent me, that thou mightest receive thy sight, and be filled with the Holy Ghost. And immediately there fell from his eyes as it had been scales: and he received sight forthwith, and arose, and was baptized" (Acts 9:17–18).

Little wonder Paul ever afterward asked of his believers, "Have ye received the Holy Ghost?" (Acts 19:2). His vision of Christ, his own assurance of salvation, his determination to endure the world—all these were confirmed, magnified, and sealed by the gift of the Holy Ghost now within him. As with the other apostles, Paul came to understand Christ's dealings with him on the way only after he had received the Spirit of Truth, the Revelator, the Comforter. And only with this gift could Peter, Paul, John, Cornelius, and any other Jew or Gentile overcome the flesh, endure to the end, and know and understand "wisdom, mercy, truth, justice, and judgment" (Moses 6:61).

And lest we err, receiving the Holy Ghost, although a gift of God, is not optional to our salvation. Without this Comforter and divine presence, we are not only left alone but sooner or later are also left unto ourselves to degrade, falter, and become devilish or, as Jacob taught, even "angels to a devil" (2 Nephi 9:9).

We either progress with this gift or retrogress without it. King Benjamin, whose words Joseph Smith had translated early on in the work on the Book of Mormon, explained: "For the natural man is an enemy to God, and has been from the fall of Adam, and will be, forever and ever, unless he yields to the enticings of the Holy Spirit, and putteth off the natural man and becometh a saint through the atonement of Christ the Lord, and becometh as a child, submissive, meek, humble, patient, full of love, willing to submit to all things which the Lord seeth fit to inflict upon him, even as a child doth submit to his father" (Mosiah 3:19).

Paul likewise taught clearly that fallen human nature is changed permanently for good only by this "grace" of God "because the love of God is shed abroad in our hearts by the Holy Ghost which is given unto us" (Romans 5:5). "For to be carnally minded is death; but to be spiritually minded is life and peace. . . . But ye are not in the flesh, but in the Spirit, if so be that the Spirit of God dwell in you. Now if any man have not the Spirit of Christ, he is none of his. And if Christ be in you, the body is dead because of sin; but the Spirit is life because of righteousness. But if the Spirit of him that raised up Jesus from the dead dwell in you, he that raised up Christ from the dead shall also quicken your mortal bodies by his Spirit that dwelleth in you" (Romans 8:6, 9–11).

It is the Holy Ghost who captures and seals the affections of the heart forever on Christ and his gospel. After all, the gospel of Christ is the consummate message of joy. As Paul repeatedly stressed, "For the kingdom of God is not meat and drink; but righteousness, and peace, and joy in the Holy Ghost" (Romans 14:17). He added, "For our gospel came not unto you in word only, but also in power, and in the Holy Ghost, and in much assurance. . . . And ye became followers of us, and of the Lord, having received the word in much affliction, with joy of the Holy Ghost" (1 Thessalonians 1:5–6).

The gospel also came with a boldness and brightness of hope. "Now the God of hope fill you with all joy and peace in believing, that ye may abound in hope, through the power of the Holy Ghost" (Romans 15:13). A clear conscience comes by the Holy Ghost (Romans 9:1), as do personal joy and sanctification (Romans 15:13, 16), the resolve to overcome the world, and the revelation of Christ, for indeed "no man can say that Jesus is the Lord, but by the Holy Ghost" (1 Corinthians 12:3).

Elder Parley P. Pratt tried to capture what it means to have this transforming power of the Holy Ghost in us in a way that transcends a mere rational look at, or casual living of, the gospel: "It quickens all the intellectual faculties, increases, enlarges, expands and purifies all the natural passions and affections[,] . . . inspires, develops, cultivates and matures all the fine-toned sympathies, joys, tastes, kindred feelings and affections of our nature. It inspires virtue, kindness, goodness, tenderness, gentleness and charity. It develops beauty of person, form and features. . . . In short, it is, as it were, marrow to the bone, joy to the heart, light to the eyes, music to the ears, and life to the whole being."[20]

Once resident within the human soul, this Spirit of Truth, "even the Comforter which was sent forth to teach the truth" (D&C 50:14), leads its host into ever-greater dimensions of truth, righteousness, and happiness. President Boyd K. Packer said, "If you can understand how the Spirit operates, you will be all right."[21]

The faith in Christ, repentance, and covenant baptism that allowed the Holy Ghost to enter into one's soul in the first place are intensified, refined, and continually reenergized with the result that the "old man" (Colossians 3:9) of sin gradually becomes "a new creature" in Christ (2 Corinthians 5:17). It is a glorious process of personal sanctification that for a few may come almost instantly but for most of us, according to our faithfulness and patient endurance, occurs over a lifetime. "That which is of God is light; and he that receiveth light, and continueth in God, receiveth more light; and that light groweth brighter and brighter until the perfect day" (D&C 50:24). "Wherefore, continue in patience until ye are perfected" (D&C 67:13).

Paul compared this transformation to the resurrection, a new life in Christ through the changing power of the Holy Ghost and with it an essential upgrade in living. "If ye then be risen with Christ, seek those things which are above, where Christ sitteth on the right hand of God," he said. "Set your affection on things above, not on things on the earth. For ye are dead, and your life is hid with Christ in God . . . seeing that ye have put off the old man with his deeds; and have put on the new man, which is renewed in knowledge after the image of him that created him" (Colossians 3:1–3, 9–10). As one Protestant writer so wisely put it: "[Christianity] is the religion of the Affections which God particularly requires."[22]

What kind of man or woman is such "a new creature" in Christ destined to become? Eventually, even like unto Christ himself. The Holy Ghost is the power to endure all things and to overcome the world. Of this truth the apostle Paul wrote: "Put on therefore, as the elect of God, holy and beloved, bowels of mercies, kindness, humbleness of mind, meekness, longsuffering; forbearing one another, and forgiving one another, if any man have a quarrel against any: even as Christ forgave you, so also do ye. And above all these things put on charity, which is the bond of perfectness. And let the peace of God rule in your hearts, to the which also ye are called in one body" (Colossians 3:12–15). Paul's reference to the elect of God as one being "called in one body" includes the continuous, enduring performance of "faith unto repentance," repentance unto baptism, baptism unto the covenant, remembrance of God through worthily partaking frequently of the sacrament, and covenant obedience unto the higher covenants of the temple, which lead to eternal life—or, in other words, "one eternal round" (Colossians 3:15; Alma 34:15; 1 Nephi 10:19).[23]

Recognizing that one can stumble and fall from the grace of Christ as shed forth in the Holy Ghost, Alma counseled his listeners that even though on the right path they must watch and pray always and endure to the end: "Humble yourselves before the Lord, and call on his holy name, and watch and pray continually, that ye may not be tempted above that which ye can bear, and thus be led by the Holy Spirit, becoming humble, meek, submissive, patient, full of love and all long-suffering; having faith on the Lord; having a hope that ye shall receive eternal life; having the love of God always in your hearts, that ye may be lifted up at the last day and enter into his rest" (Alma 13:28–29).

And from the Doctrine and Covenants, we are told, "And above all things, clothe yourselves with the bond of charity, as with a mantle, which is the bond of perfectness and peace" (D&C 88:125).

Finally, as we are taught by both Paul and Peter, the Holy Ghost is the "Holy Spirit of Promise," the great sanctifier, signifier, and sealer of our salvation and exaltation. Wrote Paul to the Corinthians, "Now he which stablisheth us with you in Christ, and hath anointed us, is God; who hath also sealed us, and given the earnest of the Spirit in our hearts" (2 Corinthians 1:21–22).

This essential doctrine of salvation he repeated to the Ephesians: "In whom also after that ye believed, ye were sealed with that holy Spirit of promise, which is the earnest of our inheritance until the redemption of the purchased possession, unto the praise of his glory" (Ephesians 1:13–14). And to Titus, he said, "According to his mercy he saved us, by the washing of regeneration [baptism], and renewing of the Holy Ghost; which he shed on us abundantly through Jesus Christ our Saviour" (Titus 3:5–6). Peter phrased it this way: "According as his divine power hath given unto us all things that pertain unto life and godliness . . . called us to glory and virtue: whereby are given unto us exceeding great and precious promises: that by these ye might be partakers of the divine nature, having escaped the corruption that is in the world through lust" (2 Peter 1:3–4).

Modern revelation attests to the truth of these first principles and the saving and sealing power of the Holy Ghost: "They are they who received the testimony of Jesus, and believed on his name and were baptized after the manner of his burial, being buried in the water in his name, and this according to the commandment which he has given—that by keeping the commandments they might be washed and cleansed from all their sins, and receive the Holy Spirit by the laying on of the hands of him who is ordained and sealed unto this power; and who overcome by faith, and are sealed by the Holy Spirit of promise, which the Father sheds forth upon all those who are just and true. They are they who are the church of the Firstborn" (D&C 76:51–54).

Peter, James, and John—Apostolic Triumvirate

Because the gift of the Holy Ghost is so critically important in God's economy of salvation, and because it was given anciently by Christ's apostles and other authorized priesthood agents, and because it must be conferred only by the laying on of hands, who more appropriate to restore the priesthood than the ancient apostles Peter, James, and John? They understood the priesthood—indeed they held the keys or governing authority over it. They had received divine commission. What is more, they had overcome the world through the gift and power of the Holy Ghost, which they had received. What better teachers of these divine truths than these chosen three?

James, the son of Zebedee and the brother of John the Beloved, is not to be confused with James, the brother of Jesus, or James, the son of Alphaeus. A fisherman, James was one of the original Twelve Apostles of the Lord and likely John's older brother because he is usually mentioned first. Along with Peter and John, James was part of that inner circle or special apostolic triumvirate that Jesus entrusted with some of the greatest and most intimate moments of his ministry: the raising of the dead (Mark 5:37), the Transfiguration on the mount (Matthew 17:1; Mark 9:2; Luke 9:28); and the Lord's agony in Gethsemane (Matthew 26:37; Mark 14:33). With the remaining eleven, James was a witness to Christ's resurrection and was a leader among the apostles. Because of that leadership, he likely was the first to be martyred—the only apostolic martyrdom referred to directly in the New Testament (Acts 12:2)—being put to death by the sword of unjust King Herod.[24] The book of James in the New Testament was likely not his but that of the brother of Christ and was probably written in Jerusalem as one of the earlier general epistles—not addressed to any specific church or person—of the New Testament.[25]

John was also a fisherman—in partnership with his older brother, James. The two brothers abruptly quit their vocation so they could follow Christ and become "fishers of men" (Matthew

4:19). If Peter was the impetuous, strong-minded leader of this inner trio of disciples, John was ever the more sensitive, soft-spoken, and self-effacing. He owned a special place in his Master's heart perhaps because of his genuine humility and modesty. Of the four Gospels, John's has long been considered the spiritual Gospel and bears within it intimate, meditative, and magisterial insights into the sermons, teachings, prayers, nature, and mission of Christ. John understood Christ's unique relationship with his Father in Heaven and the Savior's agony and sufferings in Gethsemane and on the cross, and John testified as a personal witness of His resurrection and appearance to the apostles thereafter. John's apostolic insights into the nature and mission of his beloved Master set him apart.[26]

It was this same John whom Christ, while dying on the cross, commissioned to take care of his mother. "Then saith he to the disciple, Behold thy mother! And from that hour that disciple took her unto his own home" (John 19:27)—telling evidence of the trust and esteem Christ held for John. In return for his loving care of Mary, how much did John come to learn and understand of the miraculous birth, unique childhood, divine nature, and personal mission of the Savior? Such insights prepared John to write his Gospel, his letters, and later, while imprisoned on the Isle of Patmos, his apocalyptic book of Revelation?

The apostle John received the particular blessing and commission from the resurrected Lord that he should "tarry" in the flesh till Christ's triumphant second coming (John 21:22, 23). "Then went the saying abroad among the brethren, that that disciple should not die: yet Jesus said not unto him, He shall not die; but, if I will that he tarry till I come, what is that to thee?" (John 21:23).

John himself seems purposefully vague about this blessing, but modern scripture confirms and clarifies the fact of his continuing mission as a mortal, though translated, being. Answering John's fervent prayer to have power over death so as to "bring souls unto thee," Christ gave him extended mortal life and power to "prophesy before nations, kindreds, tongues and people" (D&C 7:1–4) till the end. At that time, he will be changed "in the twinkling of an eye from mortality to immortality" (3 Nephi 28:8). Thus, at the appearance of Peter, James, and John at the Susquehanna River, John, unlike the others, was still in a mortal, albeit translated, state. Later, at Christ's millennial return, he alone, as one still in the flesh who saw and heard and touched the mortal Christ, will give final living testimony as an eyewitness of Christ's life, death, resurrection, and ascension.

Of all the Gospel writers, John owned special insights into the role and mission of the Holy Ghost. If not an eyewitness himself to Christ's baptism, he nevertheless recorded the teaching of John the Baptist that the Spirit descended "like a dove, and it abode upon him" (John 1:32). He understood that the Holy Ghost "was not yet given" the Apostles during Christ's ministry (John 7:39) but that he would send the "other Comforter" to them after his departure. "For if I go not away, the Comforter will not come unto you; but if I depart, I will send him unto you" (John 16:7). "And I will pray the Father, and he shall give you another Comforter, that he may abide with you for ever; even the spirit of truth" that "dwelleth with you, and shall be in you" (John 14:16–17). For "the Comforter, which is the Holy Ghost, whom the Father will send in my name, he shall teach you all things, and bring all things to your remembrance, whatsoever I have said unto you" (John 14:26).

It was this same John the Beloved who recorded the fulfillment of that promise after Christ's appearance as the resurrected Lord to his apostles. "Then the same day at evening, being the first day of the week, when the doors were shut where the disciples were assembled for fear of the Jews, came Jesus and stood in the midst, and saith unto them, Peace be unto you. And when he had so said, he shewed unto them his hands and his side. Then were the disciples glad, when they saw the Lord. Then said Jesus to them again, Peace be unto you: as my Father hath sent me, even so send I you. And when he had said this, he breathed on them, and saith unto them, Receive ye the Holy Ghost" (John 20:19–22). John the apostle and beloved of the Lord was therefore as great a student of the life of Christ and of the reception and operations of the Holy Ghost as any man alive—then and now.

Yet of all three apostles, it was Peter who appears to have undergone the most dramatic transformation. Variously called Simeon, Simon, Cephas, and finally Peter, meaning *rock*, this "Simon called Peter" (Matthew 4:18), brother of Andrew and likewise a fisherman, was the spokesman for the Twelve, the apostle whose name was always mentioned first among them. Their undisputed leader, Peter was the first to confess and understand the true identity of Christ. "But whom say ye that I am? And Simon Peter answered and said, Thou art the Christ, the Son of the living God" (Matthew 16:15–16). With unparalleled faith and devotion, Peter walked on the water, healed the sick, ran with the other apostles to the burial site of Christ, and entered first into the emptied tomb. Indeed, "to think of the apostles is to think first of Peter."[27] But this same pillar of faith three times denied the Savior when Christ stood before Caiaphas. "I know not the man," he swore. "And Peter remembered the word of Jesus, which said unto him, Before the cock crow, thou shalt deny me thrice. And he went out, and wept bitterly" (Matthew 26:74–75). Nonetheless, Peter, after he had received the Holy Ghost, was never the same again. Elder Richard G. Scott has said of Peter's remarkable transformation: "He [Peter] became that unwavering, rock-solid servant essential to the plan of the Father after the Crucifixion and Resurrection of the Savior. . . . Thereafter Peter rose to the full stature of his calling. He taught with power and unshakable testimony despite threats, imprisonment, and beatings. He was truly converted."[28]

Precisely when the gift of the Holy Ghost was bestowed upon the Twelve is not known. As the resurrected Christ said just before his ascension: "It is not for you to know the times or the seasons, which the Father hath put in his own power. But ye shall receive power, after that the Holy Ghost is come upon you: and ye shall be witnesses unto me both in Jerusalem, and in all Judaea, and in Samaria, and unto the uttermost part of the earth" (Acts 1:7–8).

This much is clear, however: on the day of Pentecost some time later, "there came a sound from heaven as of a rushing mighty wind," and "there appeared unto them cloven tongues like as of fire, and it sat upon each of them. And they were all filled with the Holy Ghost, and began to speak with other tongues, as the Spirit gave them utterance" (Acts 2:2–4). Thereupon Peter stood up and gave his great discourse on Jesus of Nazareth and of his resurrection and of the Holy Ghost. "Now when they heard this, they were pricked in their heart, and said unto Peter and to the rest of the apostles, Men and brethren, what shall we do? Then Peter said unto them, Repent, and be baptized every one of you in the name of Jesus Christ for the remission of sins, and ye shall receive the gift of the Holy Ghost. For the promise is unto you, and to your children, and to all that are afar off, even as many as the Lord our God shall call" (Acts 2:37–39).

A married man (Matthew 8:14), Peter became the leader of the Church, receiving visions and revelations through "the spirit of prophecy" (Revelation 19:10; Alma 43:2), healing the sick and raising the dead and speaking boldly, fearlessly, and with such unabridged power and authority of the Holy Ghost that even prison walls could not hold him. Such now was the power in this chosen vessel and oracle of the Lord "that they brought forth the sick into the streets, and laid them on beds and couches, that at the least the shadow of Peter passing by might overshadow some of them" (Acts 5:15). Because of the promised gift, he had become the "rock" of revelation (Matthew 16:18) that Christ had foretold. Elder B. H. Roberts said of Peter: "We must regard St. Peter as the head of the church after the departure of the Christ, and in close association with him St. James, and St. John; for to them throughout the New Testament is accorded a certain primacy which admits of no doubt as to their being the selected presidency of the church on earth. To St. Peter the Lord himself said: 'I [will] give unto thee the keys of the kingdom of heaven: and whatsoever [thou shalt] bind on earth shall be bound in heaven' " (Matthew 16:19).[29]

Tradition has it that unlike John, who was given the promise of remaining on the earth, Peter was martyred in Rome, where he was likely buried. While John the Revelator was given the power to remain on the earth and in the flesh till the Second Coming, what of Peter's mission? Modern revelation informs us that Christ said to Peter, "And I will make thee to minister for him [John] and for thy brother James; and unto you three I will give this power and the keys of this ministry until I come" (D&C 7:7).

President Joseph F. Smith commented upon and clarified yet another mission of the apostle Peter: "I have always believed . . . that such men as Peter and James and the twelve disciples chosen by the Savior in his time, have been engaged all the centuries that have passed since their martyrdom for the testimony of Jesus Christ, in proclaiming liberty to the captives in the spirit world and in opening their prison doors. I do not believe that they could be employed in any greater work. Their special calling and anointing of the Lord himself was to save the world, to proclaim liberty to the captives, and the opening of the prison doors to those who were bound in chains of darkness, superstition, and ignorance."[30]

Well-known in the history of Christianity is the Roman Catholic claim of Peter's being the rock upon which Christ built his church and the first in a long line of human successors and ecclesiastical leaders to the Savior himself. Latter-day Saints take a much different view. Peter's work did not end at his martyrdom but, in holding the keys of apostolic ministry, he has ever since his martyrdom been at the forefront of teaching the gospel and with it the Holy Ghost. He wrote, "Unto the spirits in prison; which sometime were disobedient, when once the longsuffering of God waited in the days of Noah, while the ark was a preparing, wherein few, that is, eight souls were saved by water. The like figure [example] whereunto even baptism doth also now save us" (1 Peter 3:19–21). And just as baptism is essential for both the living and the dead, so also is the reception of the Holy Ghost.

Conclusion

So it was that these three angelic personages—two resurrected and one translated—appeared to Joseph Smith and Oliver Cowdery to restore the higher priesthood necessary for the bestowal of the gift of the Holy Ghost. They knew very well the fourth principle of the gospel—the gift of the Holy Ghost. Just as they had endured so many afflictions and persecutions in their lifetimes in the cause of Christ through reception of him and the Comforter he sent, so too would the modern apostles Joseph and Oliver be called upon to endure many insults and injustices.

Those who had been baptized before the restored Church

was officially organized—Elder B. H. Roberts believed the number was no more than twenty-seven—were confirmed members of the Church and received the Holy Ghost.[31] That this supernal gift was now to be made available to both men and women is confirmed in the revelation Joseph received concerning his wife, Emma, who was baptized near their Harmony, Pennsylvania, home in July 1830, three months following the organization of the Church: "And thou shalt be ordained under his hand to expound scriptures, and to exhort the church, according as it shall be given thee by my Spirit. For he [Joseph] shall lay his hands upon thee, and thou shalt receive the Holy Ghost, and thy time shall be given to writing, and to learning much" (D&C 25:7–8). The gift and promptings of the Holy Ghost would empower these modern messengers to live the message of the restored gospel—enabling Joseph Smith to persist in faith in proclaiming new revelation and leading Oliver Cowdery to eventually repent and return to the restored gospel he was so instrumental in helping bring forth.

Chapter Five

HOLD OUT FAITHFUL: THE DOCTRINE OF ENDURING TO THE END

If you keep my commandments and endure to the end you shall have eternal life, which gift is the greatest of all the gifts of God.

DOCTRINE & COVENANTS 14:7

Having been well taught and carefully schooled in the first principles and ordinances of the gospel, the Prophet Joseph Smith was prepared to put in place those essentials of priesthood and church government that pertain to the subsequent principle of enduring to the end. For "as many as repent and are baptized in my name, which is Jesus Christ, and endure to the end, the same shall be saved" (D&C 18:22). As Christ instructed his apostles of old, "Ye shall be hated of all men for my name's sake: but he that endureth to the end shall be saved" (Matthew 10:22). Elements of the Restoration critical to the Savior's invitation to endure to the end include prophetic leadership and the restoration of priesthood keys, the enduring legacy of witnesses, and the establishment of the Church of Jesus Christ.

"After the Order of Melchisedec"

A study of priesthood and priesthood keys and of the establishment of permanent prophetic leadership is necessary both as benediction to all previous preparations the Prophet had received and as invocation to the pending organization of the Church in the spring of 1830. During his visit to Joseph Smith and Oliver Cowdery on 15 May 1829, John the Baptist indicated that "he acted under the direction of Peter, James and John, who held the keys of the Priesthood of Melchizedek, which Priesthood, he said, would in due time be conferred on us, and that I should be called the first Elder of the Church, and he (Oliver Cowdery) the second" (Joseph Smith–History 1:72).

Priesthood is the power of God delegated to man. It becomes a sanctifying force essential to the process of enduring righteously to the end. To the man who worthily holds the priesthood and to the family that shares in it, it is a divine power for good. To desire the priesthood is to desire a good thing because it comes with an oath and a covenant. In return for the divine blessings of sanctification and exaltation, a man promises to seek after or obtain the priesthood, to magnify his callings, to serve others unselfishly, to "live by every word that proceedeth forth from the mouth of God," and "to beware" concerning himself (D&C 84:44, 43; see also v. 33).

The ancient prophet Abraham understood this well. His quest for priesthood authority and power illustrates the importance of the priesthood in the lives and homes of Latter-day Saints. "I sought for the blessings of the fathers, and the right whereunto I should be ordained to administer the same," he wrote, not in the spirit of aspiring to office and authority but in the hopes of improving his life and centering his purpose for living more squarely upon the Lord. "Desiring also to be one who possessed great knowledge, and to be a greater follower of righteousness," he sought for the priesthood because it is an invitation to greater righteousness, more abundant living, a fuller understanding of the plan of salvation, overcoming the flesh, and a prerequisite to enduring to the end. "Desiring to receive instructions, and to keep the commandments of God, I became a rightful heir, a High Priest, holding the right belonging to the fathers" (Abraham 1:2).

Jesus Christ—as the Son of the Father, the King of Kings, and the Creator of this world and of worlds without end—does more than merely hold the priesthood: he *is* the priesthood and the fulness of all things, for "all power is given unto me in heaven and in earth" (Matthew 28:18), and "by the word of his power, when he had by himself purged our sins, sat down on the right hand of the Majesty on high" (Hebrews 1:3). The apostle Paul taught:

"For by him were all things created, that are in heaven, and that are in earth, visible and invisible, whether they be thrones, or dominions, or principalities, or powers: all things were created by him, and for him:

"And he is before all things, and by him all things consist.

"And he is the head of the body, the church: who is the beginning, the firstborn from the dead; that in all things he might have the preeminence.

"For it pleased the Father that in him should all fulness dwell" (Colossians 1:16–19).

Nevertheless, in much the same way that he condescended to be baptized by John the Baptist "to fulfil all righteousness" (Matthew 3:15), so also Jesus set the pattern by holding office within his own priesthood, specifically as "the Apostle and High Priest of our profession" (Hebrews 3:1).

The apostle Paul clearly understood this principle, as he

taught the parallel of Christ and his priesthood with the ancient Levitical high priest in carrying out the yearly covenant practice of sacrificial blood atonement for the children of Israel:

"Then verily the first covenant had also ordinances of divine service, and a worldly sanctuary.

"For there was a tabernacle made; the first, wherein was the candlestick, and the table, and the shewbread; which is called the sanctuary.

"And after the second veil, the tabernacle which is called the Holiest of all. . . .

"But into the second went the high priest alone once every year, not without blood, which he offered for himself, and for the errors of the people:

"The Holy Ghost this signifying, that the way into the holiest of all was not yet made manifest, while as the first tabernacle was yet standing. . . .

"But Christ being come an high priest of good things to come, by a greater and more perfect tabernacle, not made with hands, that is to say, not of this building;

"Neither by the blood of goats and calves, but by his own blood he entered in once into the holy place, having obtained eternal redemption for us. . . .

"And for this cause he is the mediator of the new testament" (Hebrews 9:1–15).

This perfection and redemption came not by the Levitical or Aaronic Priesthood. Paul clarified, "If therefore perfection were by the Levitical priesthood, (for under it the people received the law,) what further need was there that another priest should rise after the order of Melchisedec, and not be called after the order of Aaron? For the priesthood being changed, there is made of necessity a change also of the law. . . . For he testifieth, Thou art a priest for ever after the order of Melchisedec" (Hebrews 7:11–12, 17).

This same Jesus, the great High Priest under the new covenant and "mediator of the new testament" (Hebrews 9:15), conferred this same priesthood power and authority upon others during his ministry at Jerusalem. If under the Mosaic, or Levitical, law, others had been given divine authority to work God's will for the salvation of Israel, so under the new holy order of Christ, or Melchizedek law, others were given this authority, commencing with his twelve apostles. It was not, as Martin Luther claimed, a priesthood of all believers but a priesthood *for* all believers, for Christ carefully controlled who and why and how his authority was received:

"And he ordained twelve, that they should be with him, and that he might send them forth to preach, and to have power to heal sicknesses, and to cast out devils" (Mark 3:14–15).

"Then he called his twelve disciples together, and gave them power and authority over all devils, and to cure diseases. And he sent them to preach the kingdom of God, and to heal the sick" (Luke 9:1–2).

"Ye have not chosen me, but I have chosen you, and ordained you, that ye should go and bring forth fruit, and that your fruit should remain" (John 15:16).

Later, when Peter confronted Simon the sorcerer, who sought to purchase power by which to give the Holy Ghost, Peter rebuked him: "Thy money perish with thee, because thou hast thought that the gift of God may be purchased with money. Thou hast neither part nor lot in this matter: for thy heart is not right in the sight of God. Repent therefore of this thy wickedness" (Acts 8:20–22). Peter's rebuke came in obvious confirmation of the truth that the delegation and conferral of divine authority is predicated upon the will of God, personal righteousness, and divine inspiration.

Had the priesthood remained in force down through the ages, there would have been no apostasy and no Reformation and certainly no need of priesthood restoration in the latter days. But Paul prophesied that "grievous wolves [would] enter in among [the churches], not sparing the flock" (Acts 20:29), that "there [would] be divisions" among them (1 Corinthians 11:18), and that many would "turn away their ears from the truth . . . unto fables" (2 Timothy 4:4). To the Thessalonians he made this chilling prophecy: "Now we beseech you, brethren, by the coming of our Lord Jesus Christ, and by our gathering together unto him, that ye be not soon shaken in mind, or be troubled, neither by spirit, nor by word, nor by letter as from us, as that the day of Christ is at hand. Let no man deceive you by any means: for that day shall not come, except there come a falling away first, and that man of sin be revealed, the son of perdition; who opposeth and exalteth himself above all that is called God, or that is worshipped; so that he as God sitteth in the temple of God, shewing himself that he is God" (2 Thessalonians 2:1–4). Thus in due time Satan, sitting "in the temple of God" and in the seat of authority, would rule and reign during a long night of captivity, "shewing himself that he is God."

"The Circumference of the Apostleship"

A careful reading of scriptural text and of the statements of the earliest apostles of our time reveals that Joseph and Oliver received from Peter, James, and John something even more than priesthood authority, as great as that was. They also received the keys pertaining to and governing that priesthood. While some may think that this is an overly subtle differentiation—the priesthood vs. the keys of the priesthood—it is of great importance to distinguish between the two. The keys meant everything to the form of government in the Church, the matter of apostolic succession, and even the timing or chronology of the coming of Peter, James, and John.

If priesthood is Christ's delegated authority given unto men to perform ordinances, miracles, and other works in his stead, then keys of the priesthood represent the governing authority, the power over the priesthood, the permitting or consenting power to direct, comment, confirm, revoke, and be accountable for all matters of ecclesiastical administration and ordination. They also represent sealing powers that "whatsoever ye shall bind on earth shall be bound in heaven" (Matthew 18:18).

Just as Joseph Smith and Oliver Cowdery obtained not only the Aaronic Priesthood from John the Baptist but also the keys pertaining thereto, so later they received the keys of the apostleship from Peter, James, and John, who possessed them. While not divesting themselves of these keys and priesthood—for they will hold "this power and the keys of this ministry until I come" (D&C 7:7)—Peter, James, and John nevertheless shared them with these two mortal recipients to the blessing of the sons and daughters of God on earth. "And also with Peter, and James, and John, whom I have sent unto you, by whom I have ordained you and confirmed you to be apostles, and especial witnesses of my name, and bear the keys of your ministry and of the same things which I revealed unto them; unto whom I have committed the keys of my kingdom, and a dispensation of the gospel for the last times; and for the fulness of times, in the which I will gather together in one all things, both which are in heaven, and which are on earth" (D&C 27:12–13).

The "same things" that God had revealed unto his ancient apostles—the same powers, commissions, and endowments given unto them—were now to be entrusted to these modern apostles. Joseph and Oliver were to be more than mere disciples or followers; they were to be apostles, leaders, and directors over the work of the Lord in the final dispensation before Christ's second coming.

In the Doctrine and Covenants, the Lord speaks of Joseph and Oliver as having been "called of God, and ordained an apostle of Jesus Christ, *to be* the first [and second] elder of this church" (D&C 20:2–3; emphasis added). Their ordination to the apostleship, having been set apart and sustained by the membership at the inauguration of the Church on 6 April 1830 in Fayette, New York, preceded their calling. In fact, they could not have become the first and second elders of the Church or even have organized and established the Church without first having become apostles. This truth the other early apostles of the Restoration came to understand and tried hard to teach to others.

To the argument that Joseph Smith and Oliver Cowdery were merely disciples rather than actual apostles, Elder Parley P. Pratt responded, "Who ordained our first founders to the Apostleship, to hold the keys of the kingdom of God, in these the times of restoration? Peter, James, and John, from the eternal world."[1] Added President Heber C. Kimball, "Joseph Smith was a Prophet of God, a Seer, a Revelator, an Apostle of Jesus, and was ordained directly under the hands of Peter, James, and John."[2]

Brigham Young, as president of the Church, elaborated further on the perfect sequence of events so far discussed and the order and importance of the priesthood and its keys: "When the Lord called upon His servant Joseph, after leading him along for years until he got the plates, from a portion of which the Book of

Mormon was translated, 'By and bye,' said he, 'you are going to organize my church and establish my kingdom. I am going to have a church on the earth. All these churches you have inquired about are wrong; they have truth amongst them, but not the Priesthood. They lack a guide to direct the affairs of the Kingdom of God on the earth—that is the keys of the priesthood of the Son of God.' This tells the story. We possess the Priesthood. The Lord sent John to ordain Joseph to the Aaronic Priesthood, and when he commenced to baptize people he sent a greater power—Peter, James, and John, who ordained him to the apostleship, which is the highest office pertaining to the Kingdom of God that any man can possess on the face of the earth, for it holds the keys of the Kingdom of Heaven, and has power to dispense the blessings of the kingdom."[3]

In light of the fact that the initial Quorum of the Twelve was not selected and put into place until 1835, Brigham Young's wording—that Joseph and Oliver were ordained to the "office" of apostleship—is significant. In other words, there were apostles before there was a Quorum of the Twelve Apostles—indeed, *before* there was, or could have been, an organized Church. The argument that the government of the Church was a later self-imposition of authority to justify the claims of second-generation Church leaders—and that Peter, James, and John gave Joseph and Oliver no special governing authority—disregards reason, common sense, and the statements of many Church leaders. Said Elder Orson Pratt: "This Church never could have arisen had the Lord stopped with the mere translation of the Book of Mormon and the restoration of this lesser priesthood. It is true that with the latter we could baptize, but it does not impart the power to confer the Holy Ghost; and that this Church might have the power to administer in every ordinance of the Gospel, the apostleship was again restored, which holds all the keys, authorities and powers to administer, not only in the outward ordinances, but also to confer the spirit of the living God."[4]

One of the finest and most comprehensive statements on the nature of the apostleship and of the sequence of events culminating in the organization of the Church was given by President Brigham Young in 1853 while laying the cornerstone of the Salt Lake Temple:

"I speak thus to show you the order of the Priesthood. We will now commence with the Apostleship; where Joseph commenced. Joseph was ordained an Apostle, that you can read and understand. After he was ordained to this office, then he had the right to organize, build up the kingdom of God, for he had committed unto him the keys of the Priesthood, which is after the order of Melchizedek, the High Priesthood, which is after the order of the Son of God. And this, remember, by being ordained an Apostle.

"Could he have built up the kingdom of God without first being an Apostle? No, he never could. The keys of the Eternal Priesthood, which is after the order of the Son of God, is comprehended by being an Apostle. All the Priesthood, all the keys, all the gifts, all the endowments, and everything preparatory to entering back into the presence of the Father and the Son, is in, composed of, circumscribed by, or I might say incorporated within the circumference of the Apostleship.

"Now, who do we set, in the first place, to lay the Chief, the south east corner stone: the corner from whence light emanates to illuminate the whole fabric that is to be lighted? We begin with the First Presidency, with the Apostleship, for Joseph commenced, always, with the keys of the Apostleship; and he, by the voice of the people, presiding over the whole community of Latter-day Saints, officiated in the Apostleship, as the First President.

" . . . I know that Joseph received his Apostleship from Peter, James and John before a revelation on the subject was printed, and he never had a right to organize the Church before he was an Apostle."[5]

Corroborating Brigham Young's comments is an 1847 statement by Elder Wilford Woodruff: "The Priesthood is again restored on the earth . . . we do not receive all at once, but we receive grace for grace. When Brother Joseph received the Priesthood, he did not receive all at once but he was a prophet, seer, and revelator before he received the fullness of the priesthood and keys of the kingdom.

"He first received the Aaronic Priesthood and keys from under the hands of John the Baptist. He then had not power to lay on hands to confirm the Church, but afterwards he received the Patriarchal or Melchizedek Priesthood from under the hands of Peter, James, and John who were of the Twelve Apostles and were the Presidency when the other Apostles were absent. From those Apostles, Joseph Smith received every key, power, blessing and privilege of the highest authority of the Melchizedek Priesthood ever committed to man on the earth which they held."[6]

Consequently Joseph Smith was the first and "chief" apostle *before* he was confirmed and set apart as president of the Church. "Joseph Smith was the first Apostle of this Church, and was commanded of Jesus Christ to call and ordain other Apostles," President Young later said, adding: "These other Apostles are Apostles of Jesus Christ and of Joseph Smith the chief Apostle of this last dispensation. . . . Joseph told us that Jesus was the Christ, the Mediator between God and man, and the Saviour of the world. He told us that there was no other name in the heavens nor under the heavens, neither could there be, by which mankind could be saved in the presence of the Father, but by and through the name and ministry of Jesus Christ, and the atonement he made on Mount Calvary. Joseph also told us that the Saviour requires strict obedience to all the commandments, ordinances and laws pertaining to his kingdom, and that if we would do this we should be made partakers of all the blessings promised in his Gospel."[7]

Consistent with what Brigham Young taught his fellow apostles at Hyde Park, near Kanesville, Iowa, in December 1847 while preparing for the reorganization of the First Presidency, the pattern of succession in the presidency was laid down at the very beginning. Joseph Smith could not have become president without first being an apostle, and in his case, the first apostle, or chief elder, with the keys. Brigham Young, with "seven thunders rolling" within him,[8] said that as the senior apostle (he would become president of the Church in December 1847), he was doing nothing more than his predecessor, Joseph Smith, had done seventeen years before, for the Twelve collectively had "received my kingdom" and could govern and appoint (D&C 136:41).

During the intensive deliberations of the Quorum of the Twelve at Winter Quarters in December 1847, Brigham Young proposed that it was past time for them to reorganize the First Presidency with him, as senior apostle, as the next president and successor to Joseph Smith. Not one to campaign for office, Brigham nevertheless felt that government by a First Presidency was preferable to that of the Twelve for many scriptural and logistical reasons, efficiency being one of them. Since the apostles collectively held the keys, they had the right to reorganize. "Peter, James and John constituted a First Presidency, Joseph said so many times," Brigham Young said.[9] His convincing argument was that an election or an appointment of any other potential candidate could not preempt what was rightfully now his by ordination: "You can't make me President: I am President; you can't give me power because I [already] have it."[10] Thus the pattern of apostolic succession and of continuing prophetic leadership was established in the ordination of Joseph Smith by Peter, James, and John: the senior apostle becomes president of the Church upon his ordination as such with the unanimous approval and sustaining vote of the remaining apostles in the Quorum of the Twelve. Possessing the keys to the Melchizedek Priesthood, Joseph and Oliver were prepared to enter into the operation, ordinances, and government of that priesthood, to baptize for the remission of sins and also for admittance into the Church and to both *confer* the gift of the Holy Ghost to believers and to *confirm* them members of the Church.

Does the road wind uphill all the way?
Yes, to the very end.
Will the day's journey take the whole long day?
From morn to night, my friend.[11]

Alongside the first principles of the gospel, the doctrine of enduring to the end was laid down and set in place even before the organization of the Church: it was an expectation of all those involved in the unfolding Restoration story that their testimonies would outlive them. After his 1820 vision, Joseph Smith continued to affirm the truth of what he had experienced, a determination that led to increasing prejudice and persecution. Comparing himself to Paul of old whom many had reviled as either dishonest or mad, the Prophet Joseph also had to endure hatred, misunderstanding, and persecution for saying that he had seen a vision.

"Why persecute me for telling the truth?" he wondered. "I have actually seen a vision; and who am I that I can withstand God, or why does the world think to make me deny what I have actually seen? For I had seen a vision; I knew it, and I knew that God knew it, and I could not deny it, neither dared I do it; at least I knew that by so doing I would offend God, and come under condemnation" (Joseph Smith–History 1:25). Joseph would endure years of mounting persecution that eventually ended with his death and that of his brother Hyrum, the second witness of the Restoration, in a jail in Carthage, Illinois, in June 1844.

All Three Witnesses of the Book of Mormon—Oliver Cowdery, Martin Harris, and David Whitmer—were given the same charge to endure in their testimony as witnesses of the Restoration: "Seek to bring forth and establish my Zion. Keep my commandments in all things. And, if you keep my commandments and endure to the end you shall have eternal life, which gift is the greatest of all the gifts of God" (D&C 14:6–7).

To Oliver came the specific exhortation soon after he and Joseph had begun their translation of the Book of Mormon in Harmony, Pennsylvania: "If thou wilt do good, yea, and hold out faithful to the end, thou shalt be saved in the kingdom of God, which is the greatest of all the gifts of God; for there is no gift greater than the gift of salvation" (D&C 6:13). Although he left the Church for ten years, Oliver returned and was again baptized at Kanesville, Iowa, in 1848. Nearly forty years later, his wife, Elizabeth Whitmer Cowdery, wrote: "From the hour when the glorious vision of the Holy Messenger revealed to mortal eyes the hidden prophecies which God had promised his faithful followers should come forth in due time, until the moment when he passed away from earth, he always without one doubt or [shadow] of turning affirmed the divinity and truth of the Book of Mormon."[12]

In the revelation of chastisement given to Joseph Smith after the loss of the 116 pages in which Martin Harris was temporarily called "a wicked man" (D&C 10:7), the Lord spoke of his

Church in a spiritual sense, even before its actual organization some time later. Endurance for both Joseph and Martin was enjoined: "Behold, this is my doctrine—whosoever repenteth and cometh unto me, the same is my church. . . . And now, behold, whosoever is of my church, and endureth of my church to the end, him will I establish upon my rock, and the gates of hell shall not prevail against them" (D&C 10:67, 69).

Martin, like Oliver, later left the Church for several decades, but also like Oliver, he returned, five years before his death in 1870 at the age of ninety-two. And Martin likewise reiterated his testimony: "Yes, I did see the plates on which the Book of Mormon was written. I did see the angel, I did hear the voice of God, and I do know that Joseph Smith is a true Prophet of God, holding the keys of the Holy Priesthood."[13]

David Whitmer, the last surviving witness, gave more affidavits regarding the 1829 visit of the angel Moroni than the other two witnesses combined. A man "who declined to grow with the Church" and one "skeptical of further revelations," David Whitmer quit the Church in 1838, never to return. Nevertheless, he was the most interviewed of the Three Witnesses, and though critical of some of Joseph Smith's later teachings and policies, he continued to affirm the truth of the Book of Mormon. Perhaps he did so because he remembered distinctly the angel calling him by name and saying directly to him, "Blessed is he that keepeth His commandments."[14] Just before his death in Richmond, Missouri, in 1888, David Whitmer said: "My friend, if God ever uttered a truth, the testimony I now bear is true. I did see the angel of God, and I beheld the glory of the Lord, and he declared the record true."[15]

As were these early Church leaders, so we too are on a pilgrimage of patient endurance. President Dieter F. Uchtdorf said:

"Enduring to the end is a process filling every minute of our life, every hour, every day, from sunrise to sunrise. It is accomplished through personal discipline following the commandments of God."[16] Similarly, Elder Joseph B. Wirthlin observed: "Enduring to the end is the doctrine of continuing on the path leading to eternal life after one has entered into the path through faith, repentance, baptism, and receiving the Holy Ghost. Enduring to the end requires our whole heart or, as the Book of Mormon prophet Amaleki teaches, we must 'come unto him, and offer [our] whole souls as an offering unto him, and continue in fasting and praying, and endure to the end; and as the Lord liveth [we] will be saved.' "[17]

Enduring to the end also means even more than enduring pain, suffering, and declining health, as challenging and faith testing as these trials inevitably are. Enduring in faith can also mean letting go of long-term grievances and grudges, forgiving others, manifesting charity toward all, and abiding in Christ. President Hugh B. Brown described endurance particularly vividly: "The gospel will show us a way through and around our troubles. It promises no crown without a cross, no triumph without a battle. Remember, the storms beat upon the house built upon the rock, even as they do upon the one built on sand. True, the pathway may be strewn with rocks that bruise our feet, but when we contemplate our goal, they only tend to toughen and strengthen our resolve, and we recall that 'great works are performed not alone by strength but by perseverance.' . . . If we banish hardship we banish hardihood; out of the same door with calamity walk courage, fortitude, triumphant faith, and sacrificial love. If we abolish the cross in the world, we make impossible the Christ in man."[18]

There may yet be another kind of endurance, one closer to the original meaning of the word *endure*, which is "to hold out; suffer patiently . . . to put up with; bear; stand."[19] It may lack the glory of conquest and may not even be called victory—at least not immediately or apparently. It has everything to do with resilience, with persistence, and with a never-say-die commitment to fighting the war against sin that is forever raging within and around us. We are, after all, human, and we all sin and "come short of the glory of God" (Romans 3:23).

The apostle Paul recognized this truth when he wrote of "a thorn in the flesh, the messenger of Satan to buffet me" (2 Corinthians 12:7). Even among the greatest of us, the reach exceeds our grasp. "O wretched man that I am," bemoaned the prophet Nephi. "Yea, my heart sorroweth because of my flesh; my soul grieveth because of mine iniquities. I am encompassed about, because of the temptations and the sins which do so easily beset me. And when I desire to rejoice, my heart groaneth because of my sins; nevertheless, I know in whom I have trusted" (2 Nephi 4:17–19).

We are all subject to our frailties and the diminishment of our own cherished values. We may stumble and fall over and over again, and our weaknesses often triumph over our strengths. All around us lie addiction, discouragement, despair, and defeat—accompanied by shattered hopes and broken promises. We are repeatedly reduced to being "beggars" (Mosiah 4:19), but we remain redeemable as we become humbly reliant upon the mercy and grace and strength of Christ, "who is mighty to save" (2 Nephi 31:19). He can, over time, transform our weaknesses into strengths and our sins into righteousness, multiplying our many deficiencies into infinite capacities for good.

In praise of the Savior, the great eighteenth-century hymnist Isaac Watts penned these immortal lines:

The Lord is my light; the Lord is my strength.
I know in his might I'll conquer at length.
My weakness in mercy he covers with pow'r,
And, walking by faith, I am blest ev'ry hour.[20]

Even to the sin-bound, there is deliverance, hope, and the promise of freedom. We improve where we can, while we can, as best we can. Sometimes merely holding on, despite our weaknesses, is life's greatest victory, for "they also serve who only stand and wait."[21]

Conclusion

With everything in place—the restoration of the first principles and of the requisite authority and apostolic keys, the recent publication of the first five thousand copies of the Book of Mormon, the several statements of witnesses, and the careful schooling of a prophet now ensured—the stage was set for the organization of the Church of Jesus Christ. Pursuant to the laws of the state of New York, six men—Oliver Cowdery, Joseph Smith Jr., Hyrum Smith, Peter Whitmer Jr., Samuel H. Smith, and David Whitmer—signed the official legal certificate as the original six members of a new church.

Some sixty to seventy people, including several women and children, crowded into the small log home of Peter Whitmer Sr. in Fayette, Seneca County, New York. Joseph Smith described the solemn, yet happy occasion as follows: "Having opened the meeting by solemn prayer to our Heavenly Father, we proceeded, according to previous commandment, to call on our brethren to know whether they accepted us as their teachers in the things of the Kingdom of God, and whether they were satisfied that we should proceed and be organized as a Church according to said commandment which we had received. To these several propositions they consented by a unanimous vote. I then laid my hands upon Oliver Cowdery, and ordained him an Elder of the 'Church of Jesus Christ of Latter-day Saints;' after which, he ordained me also to the office of an Elder of said Church. . . . We then laid our hands on each individual member of the Church present, that they might receive the gift of the Holy Ghost, and be confirmed members of the Church of Christ. The Holy Ghost was poured out upon us to a very great degree—some prophesied, whilst we all praised the Lord, and rejoiced exceedingly."[22]

What had begun just ten years before and some thirty miles away in the Sacred Grove, now culminated in the establishment of the Church, never again to be taken from the earth. The time of preparation was fulfilled; the age of proclamation about to begin.

EPILOGUE

Whosoever transgresseth, and abideth not in the doctrine of Christ, hath not God. He that abideth in the doctrine of Christ, he hath both the Father and the Son.

2 John 1:9

As with holy writ, Church history is nothing if not personally instructive. The years from 1820 to 1830 remain formative and foundational to the history of The Church of Jesus Christ of Latter-day Saints. They were characterized by the visions of God and of the ministering of angels, the revelation of divine principles, the restoration of priesthood and priesthood keys, the translation and publication of the Book of Mormon, the bestowal anew of the gift of the Holy Ghost, and other preparations prerequisite to the organization and reestablishment of the Church of Christ.

They were also years of careful preparation—a school of the prophet—in "the doctrine of Christ" (2 Nephi 31:21), which constitutes the first principles and ordinances of the gospel. The integrity of the Restoration required nothing less because the message of the gospel had to be taught to and lived by the messenger of the gospel. "His claim to revelation from God, if established, leaves no doubt as to his authority to organize the Church of Christ upon the earth, and to administer authoritatively the principles and ordinances thereof," said President David O. McKay. "Thus at the very inception of this great latter-day work was laid the immovable corner-stone of Christ's Church in this dispensation, viz., the authority to officiate in the name of Jesus Christ in things pertaining to his Church."[1]

In a remarkable series of visions, Joseph Smith and those closest to him were taught the principles of faith, repentance, baptism by immersion for the remission of sins, the laying on of hands for the gift of the Holy Ghost, and enduring in righteousness. It was by faith that the powers of evil were dispelled and the heavens parted in the spring of 1820. It was by faith and repentance that Joseph Smith received continued instruction from the angel Moroni, whose office it was to declare repentance unto him and to bring forth the record hidden in Cumorah. While he was translating the Book of Mormon, it was by operation of these very principles that the heavens were opened yet again in May 1829 with the appearance of John the Baptist to Joseph Smith and Oliver Cowdery. And it was by the operation of faith and repentance unto baptism and the reception of the Holy Ghost that Peter, James, and John appeared "on the Susquehanna river, declaring themselves as possessing the keys of the kingdom, and of the dispensation of the fulness of times!" (D&C 128:20).

That Joseph Smith stumbled from time to time along his pathway of progression is readily admitted as part of his unique curriculum of instruction. Our history is a frank admission and honest awareness of his imperfections. His confessions act as a prism through which we can understand the unfolding drama of his time and mission. From the First Vision to Moroni, through years of angelic instruction, to the trials of translating and publishing the Book of Mormon, to the banks of the Susquehanna, the gospel of faith, repentance, baptism, and eventually the reception of the gift of the Holy Ghost came through real-life trial and error and instruction. As President Joseph F. Smith said: "Through Joseph Smith the gospel of repentance, baptism in water for the remission of sins, the baptism of the Holy Ghost and by fire have been restored, and the knowledge that Jesus is the Christ, the Only Begotten Son of God, is made manifest through the spirit of truth."[2] Joseph Smith's preparations were a historical laboratory in the very principles he would be called upon to teach.

During the decade of preparation from 1820 to 1830 along the road from Palmyra's Sacred Grove to Fayette's log cabin, Joseph received careful preparation. "The Lord brought to him through the ministration of angelic messengers the essential powers and principles for the re-establishment of the Lord's work among the children of men," said President Stephen L Richards. "Through the intervention of a divine messenger he was able to bring forth a whole volume of scripture and history complementing that of the Holy Bible. . . . He was shown the necessity to set up the restored kingdom of God in the earth, the steps necessary therefor, and by angelic ministers given the power and commission to perfect the establishment."[3]

Not long before his death, the venerable and much beloved John Smith, uncle to the Prophet and patriarch to the Church, voiced this little known 1851 tribute to his nephew:

"I testify that Joseph Smith was a prophet, seer, revelator, and a man of God; and what was revealed through him will prove life and salvation to those who believe and obey, or death and condemnation to all who count them as naught, and harden their hearts against the truths he preached and practiced.

"I knew him when at his mother's breast; I watched and counselled his youth; but when God spoke and taught him, I bowed to his superior knowledge; and although he was a boy, and I an old man, and his uncle, yet I was not ashamed to learn true principles from him, and like Paul at the feet of Gamaliel, drank in the truths which flowed from the prophet's lips."[4]

President Joseph F. Smith said of the Prophet: "Joseph Smith was the instrument chosen of God and endowed with his authority to restore the holy Priesthood, the power of God to bind on earth and in heaven,—the power of the Priesthood by which men may perform ordinances of the gospel of Jesus Christ for the salvation of mankind. Through Joseph Smith the gospel of repentance, baptism in water for the remission of sins, the baptism of the Holy Ghost and by fire have been restored, and the knowledge that Jesus is the Christ, the Only Begotten Son of God, is made manifest through the spirit of truth. We are obligated to this humble servant that the Lord chose to lay the foundation of this work for the ordinances of the gospel of the Son of God."[5]

He added: "I come nearer the possession of the actual knowledge that Jesus is the Christ, the Son of the living God, through the testimony of Joseph Smith . . . [because] he saw Him, . . . he heard Him, . . . he received instructions from Him, [and] he obeyed those instructions, and . . . stands before the world as the last great, actual, living, witness of the divinity of Christ's mission."[6]

As we have learned from this study, there is precedent for such training of a prophet and a great lesson to be learned. Paul the apostle, to whom Joseph Smith often compared his own visions and experiences, recognized the divine template at work in his own life: "This is a faithful saying, and worthy of all acceptation, that Christ Jesus came into the world to save sinners; of whom I am chief. Howbeit for this cause I obtained mercy, that in me first Jesus Christ might shew forth all longsuffering, for a *pattern* to them which should hereafter believe on him to life everlasting" (1 Timothy 1:15–16; emphasis added).

May it not be that we as followers of Christ have been and will be taught in much the same way? Surely, if our Father in Heaven expects us to follow this same way, he will teach us these same things. Can he expect us to live what we have not been taught? Is there not a road for all of us from Palmyra to Fayette? It may be enormously instructive to see the hand of God at work in our own lives, to ponder when, where, and how we are being taught faith, repentance, baptism unto covenant living, receiving and living by the Holy Ghost, and enduring to the end. By so doing we may begin to see the hand of God alive in us and to understand life's trials and difficulties in a whole new light of faith and endurance. We also are learning "line upon line, precept upon precept" (D&C 98:12; 2 Nephi 28:30) the things of God.

And lest we mistake, learning and applying these eternal principles are not merely good things: They are essential things. We neglect them at our own peril, as Noah declared to his unbelieving generation: "Hearken, and give heed unto my words; believe and repent of your sins and be baptized in the name of Jesus Christ, the Son of God, even as our fathers, and ye shall receive the Holy Ghost, that ye may have all things made manifest; and if ye do not this, the floods will come in upon you" (Moses 8:23–24).

John the Beloved warned: "Whosoever transgresseth, and abideth not in the doctrine of Christ, hath not God. He that abideth in the doctrine of Christ, he hath both the Father and the Son" (2 John 1:9).

Nephi in the Book of Mormon testified: "Wherefore, my beloved brethren, I know that if ye shall follow the Son, with full purpose of heart, acting no hypocrisy and no deception before God, but with real intent, repenting of your sins, witnessing unto the Father that ye are willing to take upon you the name of Christ, by baptism—yea, by following your Lord and your Savior down into the water, according to his word, behold, then shall ye receive the Holy Ghost; yea, then cometh the baptism of fire and of the Holy Ghost; and then can ye speak with the tongue of angels, and shout praises unto the Holy One of Israel" (2 Nephi 31:13).

And if, as President Thomas S. Monson has often taught, "whom the Lord calls, the Lord qualifies,"[7] then Joseph Smith, "established to be a prophet of the Lord" (1 Samuel 3:20), was well taught and carefully prepared to live the very principles he would proclaim and to be the messenger of truth and integrity for this time—a prophet in word and in deed.

NOTES

Introduction

1. Taylor, 7 Oct. 1865, *Journal of Discourses,* 11:160.
2. Compare *Times and Seasons* 3 (Mar. 1842): 706, 709. Early in 1842, John Wentworth, editor and proprietor of the *Chicago Democrat,* asked the Prophet for a "sketch of the rise, progress, persecution, and faith" of the Latter-day Saints. Though Wentworth apparently never published Joseph's response, it was printed in the *Times and Seasons* in Nauvoo in March 1842.
3. Hinckley, *Teachings of Gordon B. Hinckley,* 242.
4. Clark, *On the Way to Immortality and Eternal Life,* 122.
5. Wordsworth, *Ode: Intimations of Immortality,* stanza 9, lines 27–32.
6. Smith, *Gospel Doctrine,* 90–91.

Chapter 1
And Thus by Faith, They Did Lay Hold upon Every Good Thing

1. Said President Brigham Young of the foreordination of the Prophet Joseph: "It was decreed in the counsels of eternity, long before the foundations of the earth were laid, that he [Joseph Smith] should be the man, in the last dispensation of this world, to bring forth the word

of God to the people, and receive the fulness of the keys and power of the Priesthood of the Son of God" (*Journal of Discourses*, 7:289).

2. *Lectures on Faith*, 1:9.
3. Talmage, *Articles of Faith*, 97.
4. *Lectures on Faith*, 3:4–5.
5. Joseph Smith to Newell Knight, 20 Aug. 1830.
6. Graham, *How to Be Born Again*, 26.
7. Lewis, *Mere Christianity*, 123–24, 129.
8. Thornton and Varenne, *Essential Pope Benedict XVI*, 35.
9. This narrative may have served as a precedent for his daughter Lucy Mack Smith's later book, *History of Joseph Smith by His Mother*, and perhaps also for Joseph Smith's own history.
10. Mack, *Narrative of the Life of Solomon Mack*, 23–24. For additional insights on the writings of Solomon Mack, see Anderson, *Joseph Smith's New England Heritage*.
11. Smith, *History of Joseph Smith by His Mother*, 48.
12. Smith, *History of Joseph Smith by His Mother*, 48; see also Bushman, *Joseph Smith and the Beginnings of Mormonism*, 39. When speaking of Lehi's dream, one should, as John Henry Evans once advised, use caution: "It is possible, however, that the account of these and other 'visions' of the elder Smith is couched in Lucy's own language and written in the light of Lehi's dream of the 'tree whose fruit was desirable to make one happy' " (*Joseph Smith*, 30).
13. Smith, *History of Joseph Smith by His Mother*, 116.
14. For more on the role of women in these revivals, see Cope, "Presence of Women."
15. Smith, *Recollections of Nettleton*, 52–56, 73–74. For more on these revivals, see Porter, "Reverend George Lane," 321–40.
16. Smith, *Recollections of Nettleton*, 77.
17. *Narrative of the Revival of Religion*, 25–26.
18. *Narrative of the Revival of Religion*, 27.
19. "Letter of Rev. J. Bradley," 195–97.
20. "Letter by J. M. Peck," 194. Among the Baptist preachers likely laboring in and around Palmyra in 1820 were Solomon Goodale, Thomas Baker, Jesse Braman, Joshua Bradley, J. Hamrich, Edward Martin, and Ariel Kendrick.

21. Kendrick, "November 1817, Poultney, Vermont," 305. The Reverend Benjamin Lane wrote in a similar vein of the effect upon the youth: "Four little children, being deeply impressed with the importance of religion, made a practice of going (between school hours) into a retired grove, where they spent their time in reading and prayer. The Lord heard their infant cries, and liberated their souls from the captivity of Satan and translated them, as we have reason to believe, into the kingdom of his dear Son" ("December 12, 1817, Townsend," 304–5).
22. Backman, *Joseph Smith's First Vision*, 53–89.
23. Canton, *History of the British and Foreign Bible Society*, 1:465–66; see also Owen, *History of the Origin and First Ten Years*, 15. Canton's account was first published in the Bible Society's *Monthly Reporter*, Jan. 1867.
24. The Society for Promoting Christian Knowledge had distributed some copies of the Bible in England, Wales, India, and Arabia. The Society for the Propagation of the Gospel in Foreign Parts commenced in 1701, with special emphasis on the American colonies. The year 1750 saw the start-up of the Scottish Society for Propagating Christian Knowledge among the Poor, and in 1780 the Naval and Military Bible Society began (http://www.newadvent.org/cathen).
25. Browne, *History of the British and Foreign Bible Society*, 1:10nn1–2.
26. Browne, *History of the British and Foreign Bible Society*, 1:318.
27. Howsam, *Cheap Bibles*, 53. On the positive influence of women, the Reverend Steudel of the University of Tuebingen wrote the following in January 1820: "No gentleman could be found, who would undertake the task of going from house to house, to receive the subscriptions, and to make the necessary inquiries into the actual want of Bibles; but . . . [the ladies] immediately set to work with cheerfulness and courage, not minding the cold and even unfriendly reception which they met with here and there. . . . On entering a room whence an old woman was about to dismiss them with repulsive language, a poor girl, who had earnestly listened to their representations, rose from her spinning wheel, saying, in a cheerful tone, 'I believe I have a few halfpence in my box; most gladly will I give them for so blessed a design.' She fetched them, and they were her little all. Her conduct softened the old woman,

and she likewise came forward with a few pence" (*Sixteenth Report of the British and Foreign Bible Society 1820*, 102). Whenever possible, the societies sought to sell their Bibles rather than merely give them away.

28. Browne, *History of the British and Foreign Bible Society*, 1:76.
29. Browne, *History of the British and Foreign Bible Society*, 1:155.
30. Mundus: Gateway to missionary collections in the United Kingdom, "British and Foreign Bible Society," accessed 9 Apr. 2010 at http://www.mundus.ac.uk/cgi-bin/search?coll_id=292&inst_id=38&keyword=British %20and%20Foreign%20Bible%20Society
31. Jackson, "Joseph Smith's Cooperstown Bible, 41. For an excellent study of the history of the Bible in America, see Gutjahr, *American Bible*.
32. Dwight, *Centennial History*, 3.
33. Daniell, *Bible in English*, 594–96, 598–99, 627–29.
34. For a comprehensive and detailed study of the various American editions of the Bible, see Hills, *English Bible in America*.
35. Daniell, *Bible in English*, 639.
36. *Brief Analysis*, 63.
37. See Lacy, *Word-Carrying Giant*, 50; see also Dwight, *Centennial History*, 84; *Brief Analysis*, 45. The following report was made by an agent in Long Island, New York: "I am confident no region will be found in a Christian land where Bibles are more needed. There are here multitudes of people but just able to live, and who live and die almost as ignorant of the gospel as the Heathen. Many who observe no Sabbaths, enjoy no religious ordinances, and have no religion, and they value them not, for they have no Bibles" (Lacy, *Word-Carrying Giant*, 41).
38. "First Annual Report . . . May 8, 1817," 137–44.
39. "Fifth Report . . . May 10, 1821," 312.
40. *Brief Analysis*, 33. By 1916, after its first century, the figure stood at 115 million volumes of scripture in 164 different languages (Dwight, *Centennial History*, 521).
41. Dwight, *Centennial History*, 85. It may be worth noting that the Bible "which fed the soul of Abraham Lincoln in the Kentucky log cabin of his boyhood, was one of those cheap little Bibles imported from London" (Dwight, *Centennial History*, 3).
42. Eyring, "Prayer," 17.
43. Cannon, *Life of Joseph Smith*, 30.

44. Hinckley, *Teachings of Gordon B. Hinckley*, 188.
45. Richards, *Where Is Wisdom?* 99.
46. Hinckley, *Teachings of Gordon B. Hinckley*, 227.
47. Kimball, *Faith Precedes the Miracle*, 92–93.
48. Cannon, *Gospel Truth*, 126, from a sermon given 2 Sept. 1883; see also *Journal of Discourses*, 24:372–73.
49. Monson, *Pathways to Perfection*, 54.
50. "Unanswered Yet? The Prayer," *Hymns*, 1948, no. 286.

Chapter 2
The Office of Their Ministry Is to Call Men unto Repentance

1. Talmage, *Articles of Faith*, 109.
2. Thornton, *Essential Pope Benedict XVI*, 260–61.
3. *Messenger and Advocate* 1, no. 5 (Feb. 1835): 79.
4. Such a close reading of faith as the primary cause of the First Vision should not be the sole consideration. The Doctrine and Covenants makes clear that in his first encounter with God, Joseph Smith "received a remission of his sins" only to be later "entangled in the vanities of the world" (D&C 20:5). Likewise in Joseph's 1832 account of the First Vision, he said the Lord "spake unto me saying Joseph thy Sins are forgiven thee, go thy way [and] walk in my statutes and keep my commandments" (Backman, *Joseph Smith's First Vision*, 155–57). The line between faith and repentance is an invisible one, for they are a continuum, one leading into the other. Yet it cannot be denied that in the official account of the First Vision, Joseph's quest for forgiveness prompted his 1823 prayer in a special way.
5. For instance, in the spring of 1836 at the dedication of the Kirtland Temple, when Christ appeared before the altars of the temple, among the first words he proclaimed to Joseph Smith and Oliver Cowdery were, "Behold, your sins are forgiven you; you are clean before me; . . . lift up your heads and rejoice" (D&C 110:5). Just as faith precedes the miracle, so repentance often precedes receiving a commission.
6. "I had been tempted of the adversary and sought the plates to obtain riches and kept not the commandments that I should have an eye single to the glory of God. Therefore I was chastened and sought diligently to obtain the plates and obtained them not until I was

twenty-one years of age" (Smith, *Personal Writings*, 7; spelling and punctuation modernized).

7. Cannon, *Life of Joseph Smith*, 40–41.
8. For more on Joseph Smith's early money-digging efforts, see Porter, *Study of the Origins*, 48–49. See also Bushman, *Joseph Smith and the Beginnings of Mormonism*, 68–70; Quinn, *Early Mormonism*, 48–49; Vogel, *Joseph Smith*, 69–84.
9. Smith, *History of the Church*, 1:17.
10. To read about Martin Harris's visit to New York City, see Bennett, "Read This, I Pray Thee," 178–216; see also Kimball, "Anthon Transcript," 325–52.
11. Smith, *History of Joseph Smith by His Mother*, 168.
12. Smith, *History of Joseph Smith by His Mother*, 161.
13. Smith, *History of Joseph Smith by His Mother*, 164–66.
14. Smith, *History of Joseph Smith by His Mother*, 166. For more on the lessons Joseph Smith learned from losing the 116 pages, see Perkins, "Thou Art Still Chosen," 15–19.
15. Smith, *History of Joseph Smith by His Mother*, 174.
16. Cannon, *Life of Joseph Smith*, 55.
17. Smith, *History of Joseph Smith by His Mother*, 176.
18. Smith, *History of Joseph Smith by His Mother*, 199.
19. Smith, *History of the Church*, 1:54–55.
20. Smith, *Papers of Joseph Smith*, 1:10; spelling and punctuation modernized; also cited in Richard Lloyd Anderson, "A Brief Biography of Oliver Cowdery," in Welch and Morris, *Oliver Cowdery*, 3.
21. Oaks, "Our Strengths Can Become Our Downfall," 6.
22. Another reason Oliver may have been given the gift to translate was to validate, as a second witness, the truth of Joseph's translating efforts. "And now, behold, I give unto you, and also unto my servant Joseph, the keys of this gift, which shall bring to light this ministry; and in the mouth of two or three witnesses shall every word be established" (D&C 6:28).
23. Adkins and Adkins, *Keys of Egypt*, 84.
24. Budge, "Rosetta Stone," 4.
25. Parkinson, *Cracking Codes*, 40.
26. Emma Smith later told the experience of the translation period to her

son as follows: "I am satisfied that no man could have dictated the writing of the manuscripts unless he was inspired; for, when [I was] acting as his scribe, your father would dictate to me hour after hour; and when returning after meals or after interruptions, he would at once begin where he had left off, without either seeing the manuscript or having any portion of it read to him. This was a usual thing for him to do. It would have been improbable that a learned man could do this; and, for one so ignorant and unlearned as he was, it was simply impossible" (*Saints' Herald* 26 [1 Oct. 1879]: 290).

27. Statement of David Whitmer to William H. Kelley and G. A. Blakeslee of Gallen, Michigan, 15 Sept. 1882, in *Baden and Kelley Debate on Divine Origin of the Book of Mormon*, 186, as cited in Roberts, *Essential B. H. Roberts*, 139.
28. Roberts, *New Witnesses for God*, 2:135; 3:415.

Chapter 3
I Know the Door: Baptism by Immersion for the Remission of Sins

1. Cited in Cottle, *Reminiscences*, 16–17. Thomas Chatterton, a gifted poet who had recently and tragically died in the flower of his youth, had become a wistful and nostalgic icon of the age.
2. Cottle, *Reminiscences*, 16.
3. Bushman, *Rough Stone Rolling*, 54.
4. Newell and Tippetts, *Mormon Enigma*, 26; spelling modernized.
5. Newell and Tippetts, *Mormon Enigma*, 27.
6. Smith, *Gospel Doctrine*, 189–90.
7. Bushman, *Rough Stone Rolling*, 74.
8. Oaks, "Special Witnesses of Christ," *Ensign*, Apr. 2001, 13.
9. Lewis, *Mere Christianity*, 199.
10. Roberts, *Truth*, 470.
11. *Messenger and Advocate*, Oct. 1834, 15.
12. Smith, *Gospel Doctrine*, 189.
13. Elder B. H. Roberts believed that the angel stood "upon the banks supervising it. Surely the manner of it, and the purpose of it, would be correct when introduced under such supervision" (*Truth*, 470).
14. Smith, *Gospel Doctrine*, 192–93.
15. Roberts, *New Witnesses for God*, 1:224–26.

16. Talmage, *Articles of Faith*, 8.
17. Smith, *Doctrines of Salvation*, 3:89. Elder James E. Talmage wrote: "John the Baptist was the special preacher of [repentance], and the authorized administrator of the ordinance [of baptism] in the days immediately preceding the Savior's ministry in the flesh; and the voice of this priest of the desert stirred Jerusalem and reverberated through all Judea, proclaiming remission of sins as the fruits of acceptable baptism" (*Articles of Faith*, 122).
18. Smith, *History of the Church*, 5:258.
19. Smith, *History of the Church*, 5:260–61.
20. President Joseph Fielding Smith stated that this Elias was indeed John the Baptist (*Doctrines of Salvation*, 1:172).
21. Hinckley, *Teachings of Gordon B. Hinckley*, 553.
22. Porter, "Restoration of the Aaronic and Melchizedek Priesthoods," 33.
23. Brigham Young, President, and Willard Richards, Clerk to Oliver Cowdery, Esq.," 22 Nov. 1848; see also Welch and Morris, *Oliver Cowdery*, 338.
24. "Report to Brigham Young," 5 Apr. 1849; spelling modernized.
25. Pottawattamie High Council Minutes, 5 Nov. 1848; see also Welch and Morris, *Oliver Cowdery*, 346; spelling modernized.
26. Reuben Miller, Journal, 21 Oct. 1848, LDS Church History Library, Salt Lake City, Utah, as cited in Scott H. Faulring, "The Return of Oliver Cowdery," in Welch and Morris, *Oliver Cowdery*, 344.

Chapter 4
Have Ye Received the Holy Ghost?

1. Roberts, *Truth*, 470.
2. Addison Everett to Oliver B. Huntington, 17 Feb. 1881; spelling and grammar modernized. Additional information is found in Huntington, Diary No. 15, 44–47, where the letter is again recorded with few additional particulars; see also Addison Everett to Joseph F. Smith, 16 Jan. 1882. I am indebted to Professor Larry C. Porter for the above information. For a full discussion of the Everett letters and the restoration of the Aaronic and Melchizedek Priesthoods, see Porter, "Restoration of the Aaronic and Melchizedek Priesthoods," 30–47.
3. According to the private journal of Oliver B. Huntington, President

Wilford Woodruff once grappled with the question of the timing of the restoration of the higher priesthood. "Some people suppose that [1831] was the time that Joseph and Oliver [were] ordained to the Apostleship by Peter, James and John, thereby inferring that the Church was organized before [the] Melchizedek Priesthood was given; which is all wrong simply because some people want to criticize and find something wrong. The Melchizedek Priesthood was given before the Church was organized, in 1829 or March 1830" (Diary of Oliver B. Huntington, 3 Mar. 1883, 210–11).

4. Cannon, *Life of Joseph Smith,* 75.
5. Reuben Miller, Journal, 21 Oct. 1848, LDS Church History Library, Salt Lake City, Utah, as cited in Scott H. Faulring, "The Return of Oliver Cowdery," in Welch and Morris, *Oliver Cowdery,* 147.
6. Clark, *On the Way to Immortality and Eternal Life,* 144.
7. Orson Pratt, *Journal of Discourses,* 14:145.
8. Smith, *Gospel Doctrine,* 92.
9. Cowley, *Matthew Cowley Speaks,* 366.
10. Pratt, *Essential Orson Pratt,* 205.
11. Of the matter of the Holy Ghost being Deity, Elder B. H. Roberts wrote: "There remains to be considered the question, is the Holy Ghost God—Deity in his own right? The proof is in the fact that the Holy Ghost is an equal member of the Holy Trinity. Also in the fact that Jesus makes blasphemy against the Holy Ghost a greater sin than blasphemy against himself, for he said: 'All manner of sin and blasphemy shall be forgiven unto men: but the blasphemy against the Holy Ghost shall not be forgiven unto men. . . . Whosoever speaketh a word against the Son of man, it shall be forgiven him: but whosoever speaketh against the Holy Ghost, it shall not be forgiven him, neither in this world, neither in the world to come' (Matthew 12:31, 32; see also Mark 3:28–29). This could not be unless the Holy Ghost were Deity, and in some peculiar way so related to men, that makes this sin of blasphemy against the Holy Ghost especially heinous. It may come from the fact that the Holy Ghost has especially the function of chief witness for divine truth in the Holy Trinity" (*Truth,* 230).
12. From a sermon by Joseph Smith, 16 July 1843, in Ehat and Cook, *Words of Joseph Smith,* 230.

13. Smith, *History of the Church*, 4:42.
14. Smith, *History of the Church*, 5:27.
15. Widtsoe, *Evidences and Reconciliations*, 1:77.
16. Smith, *History of the Church*, 3:379.
17. Woodruff, *Journal of Discourses*, 13:157.
18. Talmage, *Articles of Faith*, 165.
19. Said Elder Parley P. Pratt of this physical requirement: "To impart a portion of the Holy Spirit by the touch, or by the laying on of hands; or to impart the element of life, from one animal body to another, by an authorized agent who acts in the name of God, and who is filled therewith, is as much in accordance with the laws of nature, as for water to seek its own level; air, its equilibrium; or heat and electricity, their own mediums of conveyance" (*Key to the Science of Theology*, 99).
20. Pratt, *Key to the Science of Theology*, 101.
21. Packer, "The 20-Mark Note," 6.
22. Wilberforce, *Practical View*, 72.
23. See Bednar, "Honorably Hold a Name and Standing," 98.
24. *Interpreter's Dictionary of the Bible*, 790–91; see also *Anchor Bible Dictionary*, 3:620–22; *International Standard Bible Encyclopedia*, 2:958–59.
25. Whitchurch, "Discipleship and the Epistle of James," 259–60.
26. As President Gordon B. Hinckley said: "I like to read the Gospel of John. Over sixty years ago my missionary companion and I started reading the Gospel of John which begins with that great opening statement, 'In the beginning was the Word, and the Word was with God, and the Word was God.' Our reading of [it] did something to me. And I still love to read the Gospel of John" (*Teachings of Gordon B. Hinckley*, 279).
27. *Interpreter's Dictionary*, 750.
28. Scott, "Full Conversion Brings Happiness," 24.
29. Roberts, *Truth*, 516–17.
30. Smith, *Gospel Doctrine*, 460. President Smith's insight corroborates the purpose of Latter-day Saint temple worship.
31. Roberts, *Comprehensive History*, 1:196. That many men and women were baptized and confirmed members of the Church on 6 April 1830 is a historical fact. Though Joseph Smith and Oliver Cowdery were

sustained by the membership in their leadership callings, no evidence has been found to show that they were either rebaptized or reconfirmed.

Chapter 5
Hold Out Faithful: The Doctrine of Enduring to the End

1. Parley P. Pratt, *Journal of Discourses,* 2:44.
2. Heber C. Kimball, *Journal of Discourses,* 6:256.
3. Brigham Young, *Journal of Discourses,* 12:70.
4. Orson Pratt, *Journal of Discourses,* 12:361.
5. Young, *Journal History of the Church,* 6 Apr. 1853, 8–9. President Young continued: "What comes next in the Church? I will now refer you directly to the building up of the Kingdom of God in the last days. What do we see next? Joseph as an Apostle of the Lamb, with the keys of the eternal Priesthood committed unto him by Peter, James, and John. What for? To build up the Kingdom of God on the earth. Next grows out an office pertaining to the temporal affairs of this Kingdom, the keys of which are committed to men on the earth, preparatory to its establishment. . . . We see this gigantic Apostle thus standing forth, clothed with the authority of heaven, to build up His cause on the earth" (*Journal of Discourses,* 1:134–35).
6. Woodruff, *Journal,* 15 Aug. 1847, 3:256.
7. Young, *Journal of Discourses,* 9:364–65.
8. "Minutes of a Meeting of the Twelve," 5 Dec. 1847, Brigham Young Papers, as cited in Bennett, *We'll Find the Place,* 289.
9. Minutes of a Meeting of the Twelve and Seventy.
10. "Minutes of a Meeting of the Twelve"; see also Bennett, *Mormons at the Missouri,* 210, 308.
11. Rossetti, "Uphill," 393.
12. Elizabeth Cowdery to David Whitmer, 8 Mar. 1887, in Anderson, *Investigating the Book of Mormon Witnesses,* 63.
13. Rhett Stephens James, "Martin Harris," in Garr, Cannon, and Cowan, *Encyclopedia of Latter-day Saint History,* 469–70.
14. Anderson, *Investigating the Book of Mormon Witnesses,* 70, 80.
15. Journal of Angus Cannon, 7 Jan. 1888, in Anderson, *Investigating the Book of Mormon Witnesses,* 90.
16. Uchtdorf, "Have We Not Reason to Rejoice?" 20.

17. Wirthlin, "Press On," 101.
18. Brown, "Salvation Is My Goal," *New Era,* 1974.
19. *World Book Dictionary,* s.v. "Endure," 1:699.
20. "The Lord Is My Light," *Hymns,* 1985, no. 89; emphasis added.
21. Milton, "On His Blindness," 178.
22. Smith, *History of the Church,* 1:77–79; see also Porter, *Study of the Origins,* 97–100.

Epilogue

1. McKay, "Joseph Smith," 88–89.
2. Smith, *Gospel Doctrine,* 478–79.
3. Richards, *Where Is Wisdom?* 101.
4. Young, "Written Testimony of John Smith," 123.
5. Smith, *Gospel Doctrine,* 478–79.
6. Smith, *Gospel Doctrine,* 495.
7. Monson, "Duty Calls," 44.

BIBLIOGRAPHY

Primary Sources

Ecclesiastical and Institutional Archives and Minutes of Special Meetings

"Minutes of a Meeting of the Twelve." Salt Lake City, 5 Dec. 1847. Church History Library. Digitized.

"Minutes of a Meeting of the Twelve and Seventy." Salt Lake City, 30 Nov. 1847. Church History Library. Digitized.

"Pottawattamie High Council Minutes," 1848–1851. Pottawattamie, Iowa. Church History Library. Digitized.

Journals, Diaries, Autobiographies, and Correspondence Files

Huntington, Oliver B. Diary, 3 Mar. 1883. L. Tom Perry Special Collections, Harold B. Lee Library, Brigham Young University, Provo, Utah.

———. Diary No. 15, 18 Feb. 1883. L. Tom Perry Special Collections, Harold B. Lee Library, Brigham Young University, Provo, Utah.

———. Journal No. 14. "Letter of Addison Everett to Oliver B. Huntington, 17 Feb. 1881, St. George, Utah." Recorded under date of 31

Jan. 1881. L. Tom Perry Special Collections, Harold B. Lee Library, Brigham Young University, Provo, Utah.

Smith, Joseph. "Joseph Smith to Newell Knight," 20 Aug. 1830. Joseph Smith Papers. Church History Library, Salt Lake City, Utah.

Smith, Joseph F. "Letter of Addison Everett to Joseph F. Smith," 16 Jan. 1882. Joseph F. Smith Collection. (MS 1325). Church History Library, Salt Lake City, Utah.

Young, Brigham. "Brigham Young, President, and Willard Richards, Clerk to Oliver Cowdery, Esq.," 22 Nov. 1848. Papers of Brigham Young. Church History Library, Salt Lake City, Utah.

———. A Report to Brigham Young, 5 Apr. 1849. Papers of Brigham Young. Church History Library, Salt Lake City, Utah.

———. "A Written Testimony of John Smith," 8 Nov. 1851. History of Brigham Young. Record of the Church Historian's Office. Church History Library, Salt Lake City, Utah.

Secondary Sources

Monographs

Adkins, Lesley, and Roy Adkins. *The Keys of Egypt: The Obsession to Decipher Egyptian Hieroglyphs*. New York: HarperCollins, 2000.

Anderson, Richard Lloyd. *Investigating the Book of Mormon Witnesses*. Salt Lake City: Deseret Book, 1981.

———. *Joseph Smith's New England Heritage: Influences of Grandfathers Solomon Mack and Asael Smith*. Salt Lake City: Deseret Book, 1971.

Backman, Milton V., Jr. *Joseph Smith's First Vision: The First Vision in Its Historical Context*. Salt Lake City: Bookcraft, 1971.

Bennett, Richard E. *Mormons at the Missouri: Winter Quarters, 1846–1852*. Norman, Okla.: University of Oklahoma Press, 2004.

———. *We'll Find the Place: The Mormon Exodus, 1846–1848*. Norman, Okla: University of Oklahoma Press, 2009.

A Brief Analysis of the System of the American Bible Society. New York: Daniel Fanshaw, 1830.

Browne, George. *The History of the British and Foreign Bible Society, From*

Its Institution in 1804, to the Close of Its Jubilee in 1854. 2 vols. London: Bagster and Sons, 1859.

Bushman, Richard L. *Joseph Smith and the Beginnings of Mormonism.* Urbana and Chicago: University of Illinois Press, 1984.

———. *Rough Stone Rolling.* New York: Alfred A. Knopf, 2005.

Cannon, George Q. *Gospel Truth: Discourses and Writings of President George Q. Cannon.* Edited by Jerreld L. Newquist. Salt Lake City: Deseret Book, 1974.

———. *Life of Joseph Smith the Prophet.* Salt Lake City: Deseret News, 1907.

Canton, William. A *History of the British and Foreign Bible Society.* 2 vols. London: John Murray, 1904.

Clark, J. Reuben, Jr. *On the Way to Immortality and Eternal Life.* Salt Lake City: Deseret Book, 1953.

Cottle, Joseph. *Reminiscences of Samuel Taylor Coleridge and Robert Southey.* New York: Wiley & Putnam, 1847.

Cowley, Matthew. *Matthew Cowley Speaks.* Salt Lake City: Deseret Book, 1954.

Daniell, David. *The Bible in English: Its History and Influence.* New Haven and London: Yale University Press, 2003.

Dwight, Henry Otis. *The Centennial History of the American Bible Society.* New York: Macmillan, 1916.

Evans, John Henry. *Joseph Smith, An American Prophet.* New York: Macmillan, 1933.

Graham, Billy. *How to Be Born Again.* Waco, Tex.: Word Books, 1977.

Gutjahr, Paul C. *An American Bible: A History of the Good Book in the United States, 1777–1880.* Stanford, Calif.: University of Stanford Press, 1999.

Hinckley, Gordon B. *Teachings of Gordon B. Hinckley.* Salt Lake City: Deseret Book, 1997.

Howsam, Leslie. *Cheap Bibles: Ninteenth-Century Publishing and the British Foreign Bible Society.* New York: Cambridge University Press, 1991.

Hymns. Salt Lake City: The Church of Jesus Christ of Latter-day Saints, 1948.

Hymns of The Church of Jesus Christ of Latter-day Saints. Salt Lake City: The Church of Jesus Christ of Latter-day Saints, 1985.

Kimball, Spencer W. *Faith Precedes the Miracle.* Salt Lake City: Deseret Book, 1979.

Lacy, Creighton B. *The Word-Carrying Giant: The Growth of the American Bible Society (1816–1966).* South Pasadena, Calif.: William Carey Library, ca. 1977.

The Lectures on Faith in Historical Perspective. Edited by Larry E. Dahl and Charles D. Tate Jr. Provo, Utah: Religious Studies Center, Brigham Young University, 1990.

Lewis, C. S. *Mere Christianity.* New York: Macmillan, 1977.

Mack, Solomon. *A Narrative of the Life of Solomon Mack, Containing an Account of the Many Severe Incidents He Met with During a Long Series of Years, Together with the Extraordinary Manner in Which He Was Converted to the Christian Faith.* Windsor, Vt.: Solomon Mack, 1811.

McKay, David O. "Joseph Smith—His Source of Knowledge." *Millennial Star* 85 (Feb. 8, 1923): 88–89.

———. *Gospel Ideals: Selections from the Discourses of David O. McKay.* Salt Lake City: Improvement Era, 1953.

Milton, John. "On His Blindness." In *Poems to Remember.* Edited by E. F. Kingston. Toronto: J. M. Dent and Sons, Ltd., 1963.

Monson, Thomas S. *Pathways to Perfection: Discourses of Thomas S. Monson.* Salt Lake City: Deseret Book, 1973.

Morison, Samuel Eliot. *The Great Explorers: The European Discovery of America.* New York: Oxford University Press, 1978.

A Narrative of the Revival of Religion, Within the Bounds of the Presbytery of Albany, in the Year 1820. Schenectady, N.Y.: Isaac Riggs, 1821.

Newell, Linda King, and Valeen Tippetts Avery. *Mormon Enigma: Emma Hale Smith, Prophet's Wife, "Elect Lady," Polygamy's Foe, 1804–1879.* Garden City, N.Y.: Doubleday, 1984.

Owen, John. *The History of the Origin and First Ten Years of the British and Foreign Bible Society.* New York: James Eastburn & Co., 1817.

Parkinson, R. B. *Cracking Codes: The Rosetta Stone and Decipherment.* Berkeley, Calif.: University of California Press, 1999.

Porter, Larry C. *A Study of the Origins of The Church of Jesus Christ of Latter-day Saints in the States of New York and Pennsylvania*. Provo, Utah: Joseph Fielding Smith Institute for Latter-day Saint History and BYU Studies, 2000.

Pratt, Orson. *The Essential Orson Pratt*. Edited by David J. Whittaker. Salt Lake City: Signature Books, 1991.

Pratt, Parley P. *Key to the Science of Theology*. Salt Lake City: Deseret Book, 1966.

Quinn, D. Michael. *Early Mormonism and the Magic World View*. Salt Lake City: Signature Books, 1998.

Richards, Stephen L. *Where Is Wisdom? Addresses of President Stephen L Richards*. Salt Lake City: Deseret Book, 1955.

Roberts, B. H. *A Comprehensive History of The Church of Jesus Christ of Latter-day Saints*. 6 vols. Salt Lake City: Deseret News Press, 1930.

———. *The Essential B. H. Roberts*. Edited by Brigham D. Madsen. Salt Lake City: Signature Books, 1999.

———. *New Witnesses for God*. 3 vols. Salt Lake City: The Church of Jesus Christ of Latter-day Saints, 1909.

———. *The Truth, the Way, the Life*. Provo, Utah: BYU Studies, 1994.

Rossetti, Christina. "Uphill." In *Poems to Remember*. Edited by E. F. Kingston. Toronto: J. M. Dent and Sons, Ltd., 1963.

Sixteenth Report of the British and Foreign Bible Society, 1820. London: Benjamin Beasley, 1820.

Smith, Joseph, Jr. *History of The Church of Jesus Christ of Latter-day Saints*. Edited by B. H. Roberts. 2d ed. rev. 7 vols. Salt Lake City: The Church of Jesus Christ of Latter-day Saints, 1932–51.

———. *Joseph Smith* [manual]. A volume in Teachings of Presidents of the Church series. Salt Lake City: Intellectual Reserve, 2007.

———. *Lectures on Faith*. Salt Lake City: Deseret Book, 1985.

———. *Papers of Joseph Smith*. Edited by Dean C. Jessee. 2 vols. Salt Lake City: Deseret Book, 1989–92.

———. *Personal Writings of Joseph Smith*. Edited by Dean C. Jessee. 2d ed. Salt Lake City: Deseret Book, 2002.

Smith, Joseph F. *Gospel Doctrine*. Salt Lake City: Deseret News, 1919.

Smith, Joseph Fielding. *Doctrines of Salvation: Sermons and Writings of Joseph Fielding Smith.* Compiled by Bruce R. McConkie. 3 vols. Salt Lake City: Bookcraft, 1954–56.

Smith, Lucy Mack. *The Revised and Enhanced History of Joseph Smith by His Mother.* Edited by Scot Facer Proctor and Maurine Jensen Proctor. Salt Lake City: Bookcraft, 1996.

Smith, Reverend R. *Recollections of Nettleton, and the Great Revival of 1820.* Albany, N.Y.: E. H. Pease & Co., 1848.

Talmage, James E. *A Study of the Articles of Faith, Being a Consideration of the Principal Doctrines of The Church of Jesus Christ of Latter-day Saints.* Salt Lake City: The Church of Jesus Christ of Latter-day Saints, 1952.

Thacher, John Boyd. *Christopher Columbus: His Life, His Work, His Remains.* Vol. 1. New York: G. Putnam's Sons, 1903.

Thornton, John F., and Susan B. Varenne, eds. *The Essential Pope Benedict XVI: His Central Writings and Speeches.* New York: HarperCollins, 2008.

Vogel, Dan. *Joseph Smith: The Making of a Prophet.* Salt Lake City: Signature Books, 2004.

Welch, John W., and Larry E. Morris, eds. *Oliver Cowdery: Scribe, Elder, Witness.* Provo, Utah: Neal A. Maxwell Institute for Religious Scholarship, Brigham Young University, 2006.

Widtsoe, John A. *Evidences and Reconciliations.* 3 vols. Salt Lake City: Bookcraft, 1960.

Wilberforce, William. *A Practical View of Real Christianity.* London: T. Cadell and W. Davies, 1811.

Woodruff, Wilford. *Journal of Wilford Woodruff, 1833–1898.* 7 vols. Edited by Scott G. Kenney. Salt Lake City: Signature Press, 1983.

Wordsworth, William. *Ode: Intimations of Immortality from Recollections of Early Childhood.*

The World Book Dictionary. 2 vols. Chicago: World Book, 2000.

Historical Compilations and Anthologies

Brigham Young Papers. Church History Library. The Church of Jesus Christ of Latter-day Saints, Salt Lake City, Utah.

Bromiley, Geoffrey W., ed. *The International Standard Bible Encyclopedia.* 4 vols. Grand Rapids, Mich.: Eerdmans, 1982.

Ehat, Andrew F., and Lyndon W. Cook, eds. *The Words of Joseph Smith: The Contemporary Accounts of the Nauvoo Discourses of the Prophet Joseph.* Provo, Utah: Brigham Young University, 1980.

Freedman, David Noel, ed. *The Anchor Bible Dictionary.* 6 vols. New York: Doubleday, 1992.

Garr, Arnold K., Donald Q. Cannon, and Richard O. Cowan. *Encyclopedia of Latter-day Saint History.* Salt Lake City: Deseret Book, 2000.

Hills, Margaret T., ed. *The English Bible in America: A Bibliography of Editions of the Bible and the New Testament Published in America 1777–1957.* New York: American Bible Society, 1962.

The Interpreter's Dictionary of the Bible. 26 vols. Nashville: Abingdon Press. 1962–76.

Journal of Discourses. 26 vols. Liverpool: Latter-day Saints' Book Depot, 1854–86.

The Journal History of the Church. Edited by Andrew Jenson. 7 vols. Salt Lake City: Historical Department, The Church of Jesus Christ of Latter-day Saints, 1906.

Periodical Literature and Dissertations

Bednar, David A. "Honorably Hold a Name and Standing." *Ensign,* May 2009, 97–100.

Bennett, Richard E. "'Read This, I Pray Thee': Martin Harris and the Three Wise Men of the East." *Journal of Mormon History* 36 (Winter 2010): 178–216.

Brown, Hugh B. "The Message: Salvation Is My Goal." *New Era,* Dec. 1974, 4–7.

Cope, Rachel. "The Presence of Women in the Revival Movements of the Second Great Awakening." Ph.D. diss., Syracuse University, 2007.

Eyring, Henry B. "Prayer," *Ensign,* Nov. 2001, 15–17.

Jackson, Kent P. "Joseph Smith's Cooperstown Bible: The Historical Context of the Bible Used in the Joseph Smith Translation." *BYU Studies* 40, no. 1 (2001): 41–70.

Kimball, Stanley. "The Anthon Transcript: People, Primary Sources, and Problems." *BYU Studies* 10 (Spring 1970): 325–252.

Monson, Thomas S. "Duty Calls." *Ensign,* May 1996, 43–46.

Oaks, Dallin H. "Our Strengths Can Become Our Downfall." In *Devotional and Fireside Speeches, 1991–92.* Provo, Utah: Brigham Young University Press, 1992, 107–15.

Packer, Boyd K. "The 20-Mark Note." *New Era,* June 2009, 2–6.

Perkins, Keith W. "Thou Art Still Chosen." *Ensign,* Jan. 1993, 15–19.

Porter, Larry C. "The Restoration of the Aaronic and Melchizedek Priesthoods." *Ensign,* Dec. 1996, 30–47.

———. "Reverend George Lane—Good 'Gifts,' Much 'Grace,' and Marked 'Usefulness.' " *BYU Studies* 9, no. 3 (Spring 1969): 321–40.

Scott, Richard G. "Full Conversion Brings Happiness." *Ensign,* May 2002, 24–26.

"Special Witnesses of Christ." *Ensign,* Apr. 2001, 2–21.

Uchtdorf, Dieter F. "Have We Not Reason to Rejoice?" *Ensign,* Nov. 2007, 18–21.

Whitchurch, David M. "Discipleship and the Epistle of James." In *Go Ye into All the World: Messages of the New Testament Apostles. The 31st Annual Sidney B. Sperry Symposium.* Salt Lake City: Deseret Book, 2002, 259–60.

Wirthlin, Joseph B. "Press On." *Ensign,* Nov. 2004, 101–4.

Newspapers, Magazines, and Historical Pamphlets

Budge, E. A. Wallis. "The Rosetta Stone." Published by the Trustees of the British Museum. London: Harrison and Sons Ltd., 1968.

"Fifth Report of the American Bible Society, Presented at the Annual Meeting, May 10, 1821." *Methodist Magazine,* Aug. 1821, 312.

"The First Annual Report of the Board of Managers of the American Bible Society, presented May 8, 1817." *Evangelical Guardian and Review,* July 1817, 137–44.

Kendrick, Rev. Clark. "November 1817, Poultney, Vermont." *The American Baptist Magazine and Missionary Intelligencer.* Mar. 1818, 305.

Lane, Rev. Benjamin. “December 12, 1817, Townsend.” *The American Baptist Magazine and Missionary Intelligencer.* Mar. 1818, 304–5.

“Letter by J. M. Peck, Litchfield, Connecticut, July 16, 1817.” *The American Baptist Magazine and Missionary Intelligencer.* Sept. 1817, 194.

“Letter of Rev. J. Bradley, Genesee County, New York, 20 July 1820.” *The American Baptist Magazine and Missionary Intelligencer.* Sept. 1821, 195–97.

McKay, David O. “Joseph Smith—His Source of Knowledge,” *Millennial Star* 85 (Feb. 8, 1923): 88–89.

Messenger and Advocate. Kirtland, Ohio, 1834–37.

The Saints' Herald. Plano, Illinois, 1872–1881.

Times and Seasons. Nauvoo, Illinois, 1839–46.

Web Sites

“British and Foreign Bible Society's Library.” Cambridge University Library. http//www.mundus.ac.uk/cats/.

INDEX